ArchiMate® 1.0 Specificatio

Other publications by Van Haren Publishing

Van Haren Publishing (VHP) specializes in titles on Best Practices, methods and standards within four domains:
- IT management,
- Architecture (Enterprise and IT),
- Business management and
- Project management

These publications are grouped in series: *ITSM Library, Best Practice and IT Management Topics*. VHP is also publisher on behalf of leading companies and institutions: The Open Group, IPMA-NL, PMI-NL, CA, Getronics, Pink Elephant.

Topics are (per domain):

IT (Service) Management / IT Governance	Architecture (Enterprise and IT)	Project/Programme/ Risk Management
ASL	Archimate	A4 Project management
BiSL	GEA	ICB / NCB
CATS	TOGAF™	MINCE®
CMMI		M_o_R®
CoBiT	**Business Management**	MSP
ISO 17799	EFQM	PMBoK
ISO 27001	ISA-95	PRINCE2®
ISO/IEC 20000	ISO 9000	
ISPL	ISO 9001:2000	
IT Service CMM	SixSigma	
ITIL® V2	SOX	
ITIL® V3	SqEME®	
ITSM		
MOF		
MSF		

For the latest information on VHP publications, visit our website: www.vanharen.net.

ArchiMate® 1.0 Specification

THE *Open* GROUP

www.opengroup.org

Van Haren
PUBLISHING

Colofon

Title: **ArchiMate® 1.0 Specification**

A publication of: The Open Group

Publisher: Van Haren Publishing, Zaltbommel, www.vanharen.net

ISBN: 978 90 8753 502 5

Print: First edition, first impression, April 2009

Layout and design: CO2 Premedia, Amersfoort-NL

Copyright: © 2009, The Open Group

For any further enquiries about Van Haren Publishing, please send an e-mail to: info@vanharen.net

Trademarks

Comments relating to the material contained in this document may be submitted by email to: ogspecs@opengroup.org

Contents

Preface

The Open Group

The Open Group is a vendor-neutral and technology-neutral consortium, whose vision of Boundaryless Information Flow™ will enable access to integrated information within and between enterprises based on open standards and global interoperability. The Open Group works with customers, suppliers, consortia, and other standards bodies. Its role is to capture, understand, and address current and emerging requirements, establish policies, and share best practices; to facilitate interoperability, develop consensus, and evolve and integrate specifications and Open Source technologies; to offer a comprehensive set of services to enhance the operational efficiency of consortia; and to operate the industry's premier certification service, including UNIX® certification.

Further information on The Open Group is available at www.opengroup.org.

The Open Group has over 15 years' experience in developing and operating certification programs and has extensive experience developing and facilitating industry adoption of test suites used to validate conformance to an open standard or specification.

More information is available at www.opengroup.org/certification.

The Open Group publishes a wide range of technical documentation, the main part of which is focused on development of Technical and Product Standards and Guides, but which also includes white papers, technical studies, branding and testing documentation, and business titles. Full details and a catalog are available at www.opengroup.org/bookstore.

As with all *live* documents, Technical Standards and Specifications require revision to align with new developments and associated international standards. To distinguish between revised specifications which are fully backwards-compatible and those which are not:

- A new *Version* indicates there is no change to the definitive information contained in the previous publication of that title, but additions/extensions are included. As such, it *replaces* the previous publication.

- A new *Issue* indicates there is substantive change to the definitive information contained in the previous publication of that title, and there may also be additions/extensions. As such, both previous and new documents are maintained as current publications.

Readers should note that updates – in the form of Corrigenda – may apply to any publication. This information is published at www.opengroup.org/corrigenda.

This Document

This document is the ArchiMate 1.0 Specification, an Open Group Technical Standard.

Trademarks

Boundaryless Information Flow™ and TOGAF™ are trademarks and Making Standards Work®, The Open Group®, UNIX®, and the "X" device are registered trademarks of The Open Group in the United States and other countries.

ArchiMate® is a registered trademark of The Open Group.

Java™ is a trademark of Sun Microsystems, Inc. in the United States and other countries.

MDA®, Model Driven Architecture®, OMG®, and UML® are registered trademarks and BPMN™, Business Process Modeling Notation™, MOF™, and Unified Modeling Language™ are trademarks of the Object Management Group.

Telelogic™ is a trademark of Telelogic AB.

The Open Group acknowledges that there may be other brand, company, and product names used in this document that may be covered by trademark protection and advises the reader to verify them independently.

Acknowledgements

The Open Group gratefully acknowledges the contribution of the following people in the development of this Technical Standard:

- Maria-Eugenia Iacob, University of Twente
- Henk Jonkers, BiZZdesign BV
- Marc M. Lankhorst, Telematica Instituut[1]
- Erik Proper, Radboud University Nijmegen & Capgemini

The results presented in this Technical Standard have largely been produced during the ArchiMate project, and The Open Group gratefully acknowledges the contribution of the many people – former members of the project team – who have contributed to them.

The ArchiMate project comprised the following organizations:

- ABN AMRO
- Centrum voor Wiskunde en Informatica
- Dutch Tax and Customs Administration
- Leiden Institute of Advanced Computer Science
- Ordina
- Radboud Universiteit Nijmegen
- Stichting Pensioenfonds ABP
- Telematica Instituut[1]

The Open Group and ArchiMate project team would like to thank in particular the following individuals for their support and contribution to this Technical Standard:

- The Board members of the ArchiMate Foundation
- Mary Beijleveld, UWV
- Adrian Campbell, Ingenia Consulting
- Jos van Hillegersberg, University of Twente
- Andrew Josey, The Open Group
- Louw Labuschagne, Real IRM
- Daniel Moody, University of Twente
- Henk Volbeda, Sogeti
- Egon Willemsz, UWV

---

1 From April 2009, Telematica Instituut is called NOVAY

Referenced Documents

The following documents are referenced in this Technical Standard:

[1]   Enterprise Architecture as Strategy, J.W. Ross, P. Well, D.C. Robertson, Harvard Business School Press, 2006.

[2]   ISO/IEC 42010:2007, Systems and Software Engineering – Recommended Practice for Architectural Description of Software-Intensive Systems, Edition 1.

[3]   Enterprise Architecture at Work: Modeling, Communication, and Analysis, M.M. Lankhorst et al, Springer, 2005.

[4]   The Open Group Architecture Framework TOGAF, Version 9, 2009.

[5]   A Framework for Information Systems Architecture, J.A. Zachman, IBM Systems Journal, Volume 26, No. 3, pp. 276–292, 1987.

[6]   ISO/IEC JTC 1/SC 7, Information Technology – Open Distributed Processing – Reference Model – Enterprise Language, October 2006.

[7]   ITU Recommendation X.901 | ISO/IEC 10746-1:1998, Information Technology – Open Distributed Processing – Reference Model – Part 1: Overview, International Telecommunication Union, 1996.

[8]   Unified Modeling Language: Infrastructure, Version 2.0 (formal/05-05-05), Object Management Group, March 2006.

[9]   Extending and Formalizing the Framework for Information Systems Architecture, J.F. Sowa, J.A. Zachman,, IBM Systems Journal, Volume 31, No. 3, pp. 590-616, 1992.

[10]   Enterprise Ontology: Theory and Methodology, J.L.G. Dietz, Springer, 2006.

[11]   Magic Quadrant for Enterprise Architecture Tools IQ06G, A. James, R.A. Handler, Gartner Research Report G00138197, 2006.

[12]   Unified Modeling Language: Superstructure, Version 2.0 (formal/05-07-04), Object Management Group, August 2005.

[13]   A Business Process Design Language, H. Eertink, W. Janssen, P. Oude Luttighuis, W. Teeuw, C. Vissers, in Proceedings of the First World Congress on Formal Methods, Toulouse, France, September 1999.

[14]   Enterprise Business Architecture: The Formal Link between Strategy and Results, R. Whittle, C.B. Myrick, CRC Press, 2004.

[15]   Composition of Relations in Enterprise Architecture, R.v. Buuren, H. Jonkers, M.E. Iacob, P. Strating, in Proceedings of the Second International Conference on Graph Transformation, pp. 39–53, Edited by H. Ehrig et al, Rome, Italy, 2004.

[16] Viewpoints: A Framework for Integrating Multiple Perspectives in System Development, A. Finkelstein, J. Kramer, B. Nuseibeh, L. Finkelstein, M. Goedicke, in International Journal on Software Engineering and Knowledge Engineering, Volume 2, No. 1, pp. 31–58, 1992.

[17] Viewpoints for Requirements Definition, G. Kotonya, I. Sommerville, IEE/BCS Software Engineering Journal, Volume 7, No. 6, pp. 375–387, November 1992.

[18] Paradigm Shift – The New Promise of Information Technology, D. Tapscott, A. Caston, New York: McGraw-Hill, 1993.

[19] The 4+1 View Model of Architecture, P.B. Kruchten, IEEE Software, Volume 12, No. 6, pp. 42–50, 1995.

[20] Model-Driven Architecture: Applying MDA to Enterprise Computing, D. Frankel, Wiley, 2003.

[21] Performance and Cost Analysis of Service-Oriented Enterprise Architectures, H. Jonkers, M. E. Iacob, in Global Implications of Modern Enterprise Information Systems: Technologies and Applications, Edited by A. Gunasekaran, IGI Global, 2009.

[22] A Model-Driven Approach for the Rule-Based Specification of Services, M.E. Iacob, H. Jonkers, in Proceedings of the 12th IEEE International EDOC Conference, Munich, Germany, September 2008.

[23] Petri Nets: Properties, Analysis, and Applications, T. Murata, in Proceedings of the IEEE, Volume 77, No. 4, pp. 541–580, April 1989.

[24] Business Dynamics: Systems Thinking and Modeling for a Complex World, J.D. Sterman, McGraw-Hill, 2000.

[25] Operations Research: An Introduction, A.H. Taha, Prentice-Hall, 2006.

[26] Business Process Modeling Notation Specification (dtc/06-02-01), Object Management Group, February 2006.

[27] Business Motivation Model (BMM) Specification (dtc/2006-08-03), Object Management Group, August 2006.

[28] Semantics of Business Vocabulary and Business Rules (SBVR), Version 1.0 (formal/08-01-02), Object Management Group, January 2008.

[29] Business Process Definition Metamodel (BPDM) (bmi/2007-03-01), Object Management Group, March 2007.

[30] Towards Modeling and Reasoning Support for Early-Phase Requirements Engineering, E. Yu, in Proceedings of the Third IEEE International Symposium on Requirements Engineering, pp. 226–235, Washington, DC, January 1997.

[31] E3-Value: Design and Evaluation of e-Business Models, J. Gordijn, H. Akkermans, IEEE Intelligent Systems, Volume 16, No. 4, pp. 11–17, 2001.

[32] Meta Object Facility (MOF) 2.0 Query/View/Transformation Specification (formal/2008-04-03), Object Management Group, April 2008.

[33] DoD Architecture Framework (DoDAF), Version 1.5, Volume II: Product Descriptions, US Department of Defense, April 2007.

[34] FEA Consolidated Reference Model, Version 2.3, US Office of Management and Budget, 2007.

[35] CBDI-SAE Meta Model for SOA Version 2.0, J. Dodd et al, Everware-DBDI, Inc., 2007.

Chapter 1

Introduction

An architecture is typically developed because key people have concerns that need to be addressed by the business and IT systems within the organization. Such people are commonly referred to as the "stakeholders" in the system. The role of the architect is to address these concerns, by identifying and refining the requirements that the stakeholders have, developing views of the architecture that show how the concerns and the requirements are going to be addressed, and by showing the trade-offs that are going to be made in reconciling the potentially conflicting concerns of different stakeholders. Without the architecture, it is unlikely that all the concerns and requirements will be considered and met.

Architecture descriptions are formal descriptions of an information system, organized in a way that supports reasoning about the structural and behavioral properties of the system and its evolution. They define the components or building blocks that make up the overall information system, and provide a plan from which products can be procured, and subsystems developed, that will work together to implement the overall system. It thus enables you to manage your overall IT investment in a way that meets the needs of your business.

To provide a uniform representation for such architecture descriptions, the ArchiMate enterprise architecture modeling language has been developed. It offers an integrated architectural approach that describes and visualizes the different architecture domains and their underlying relations and dependencies. In a short time, ArchiMate has become the open standard for architecture modeling in the Netherlands, it is also fairly well known in the international enterprise architecture community, and recently it has been brought under the aegis of The Open Group.

ArchiMate is a lightweight and scalable language in several respects:
- Its architecture framework is simple but comprehensive enough to provide a good structuring mechanism for architecture domains, layers, and aspects.

- The language incorporates modern ideas of the "service orientation" paradigm that promotes a new organizing principle in terms of (business, application, and infrastructure) services for organizations, with far-reaching consequences for their enterprise architecture.
- Although it intentionally resembles the Unified Modeling Language (UML), the ArchiMate modeling notation is intuitive and much lighter than currently proposed by UML 2.0. Nevertheless, the language is expressive enough to allow for the modeling of all layers (business, application, and technology infrastructure) and all aspects (structure, behavior, and information) of an organization in an integrated way.
- The two enterprise architecture standards of The Open Group – TOGAF and ArchiMate – complement each other and can be used well in combination.
- Finally, tool support for the ArchiMate language is already commercially available (from BiZZdesign, IDS Scheer, Casewise, Telelogic, and others).

The goal of this Technical Standard is to provide the first official and complete specification of the ArchiMate standard under the flag of The Open Group.

This specification contains the formal definition of ArchiMate as a visual design language with adequate concepts for specifying inter-related architectures, and specific viewpoints for selected stakeholders. This is complemented by some considerations regarding language extension mechanisms, analysis, and methodological support. Furthermore, this document is accompanied by a separate document, in which certification and governance procedures surrounding the specification are specified.

1.1 Intended Audience

The intended audience of this Technical Standard is threefold:

- Enterprise architecture practitioners, such as architects (application, information, process, infrastructure, products/services, and, obviously, enterprise architects), senior and operational management, project leaders, and anyone committed to work within the reference framework defined by the enterprise architecture. It is assumed that the reader has a certain skill level and is effectively committed to enterprise architecture. Such a person is most likely to be the architect – that is, someone who has affinity with modeling techniques, knows his way around the organization, and is familiar with information technology.

- Those who intend to implement ArchiMate in a software tool. They will find a complete and detailed description of the language in this document.
- The academic community, on which we rely for amending and improving the language based on state-of-the-art research results in the architecture field.

1.2 Structure

The structure of this Technical Standard is as follows:

- Chapter 1, Introduction (this chapter)
- Chapter 2, Enterprise Architecture, makes the case for enterprise architecture and for the necessity of a modeling standard for enterprise architecture.
- Chapter 3, Language Structure, presents some general ideas, principles, and assumptions underlying the development of the ArchiMate metamodel and introduces the ArchiMate framework.
- Chapter 4, Business Layer, covers the definition and usage of the business layer concept, together with examples.
- Chapter 5, Application Layer, covers the definition and usage of the application layer concept, together with examples.
- Chapter 6, Technology Layer, covers the definition and usage of the technical infrastructure layer concept, together with examples.
- Chapters 7, Cross-Layer Dependencies, and Chapter 8, Relationships, cover the definition of relationship concepts in a similar way.
- Chapter 9, Architecture Viewpoints, presents and clarifies a set of architecture viewpoints, developed in ArchiMate based on practical experience. All ArchiMate viewpoints are described in detail. For each viewpoint the comprised concepts and relations, the guidelines for the viewpoint use, and the goal and target group and of the viewpoint are specified. Furthermore, each viewpoint description contains example models.
- Chapter 10, Language Extension Mechanisms, handles about extending and/or specializing the ArchiMate core language for specialized or domain-specific purposes.
- Chapter 11, Future Directions, identifies extensions and directions for developments in the next versions of the language.

Chapter 2

Enterprise Architecture

2.1 Why Enterprise Architecture?

The primary reason for developing an enterprise architecture is to support the business by providing the fundamental technology and process structure for an IT strategy. Further, it details the structure and relationships of the enterprise, its business models, the way an organization will work, and how and in what way information, information systems, and technology will support the organization's business objectives and goals. This makes IT a responsive asset for a successful modern business strategy.

Today's CEOs know that the effective management and exploitation of information through IT is the key to business success, and the indispensable means to achieving competitive advantage. An enterprise architecture addresses this need, by providing a strategic context for the evolution of the IT system in response to the constantly changing needs of the business environment.

Furthermore, a good enterprise architecture enables you to achieve the right balance between IT efficiency and business innovation; in essence, it aligns IT with the business. It allows individual business units to innovate safely in their pursuit of competitive advantage. At the same time, it assures the needs of the organization for an integrated IT strategy, permitting the closest possible synergy across the extended enterprise.

The technical advantages that result from a good enterprise architecture bring important business benefits, which are clearly visible in the bottom line:
- A more efficient IT operation:
  - Lower software development, support, and maintenance costs
  - Increased portability of applications
  - Improved interoperability and easier system and network management
  - Improved ability to address critical enterprise-wide issues like security
  - Easier upgrade and exchange of system components

- Better return on existing investment, reduced risk for future investment:
    - Reduced complexity in IT infrastructure
    - Maximum return on investment in existing IT infrastructure
    - The flexibility to make, buy, or outsource IT solutions
    - Reduced risk overall in new investment, and the cost of IT ownership
- Faster, simpler, and cheaper procurement:
    - Buying decisions are simpler, because the information governing procurement is readily available in a coherent plan
    - The procurement process is faster – maximizing procurement speed and flexibility without sacrificing architectural coherence

Using an architecture framework will speed up and simplify architecture development, and communication with non-architects, ensuring more complete coverage and understanding of the designed solution. The additional understanding across the enterprise enables faster response to changing business needs.

2.2 Definitions

A good definition of *enterprise* in the context of this Technical Standard is any collection of organizations that has a common set of goals and/or a single bottom line. In that sense, an enterprise can be a government agency, a whole corporation, a division of a corporation, a single department, or a chain of geographically distant organizations linked together by common ownership.

The term "enterprise" in the context of "enterprise architecture" can be used to denote both an entire enterprise, encompassing all of its information systems, and a specific domain within the enterprise. In both cases, the architecture crosses multiple systems, and multiple functional groups within the enterprise.

The definition of an *architecture* used in ISO/IEC 42010:2007 [2] is:

"The fundamental organization of a system, embodied in its components, their relationships to each other and the environment, and the principles governing its design and evolution."

As in TOGAF, ArchiMate embraces but does not strictly adhere to ISO/IEC 42010:2007 terminology [2]. We use "architecture" in two different meanings, depending on its contextual usage:

1. A formal description of a system, or a detailed plan of the system at component level to guide its implementation.
2. The structure of components, their inter-relationships, and the principles and guidelines governing their design and evolution over time.

We endeavor to strike a balance between promoting the concepts and terminology of ISO/IEC 42010:2007 – ensuring that our usage of terms is consistent with the standard – and retaining other commonly accepted terminology that is familiar to the majority of the ArchiMate and TOGAF readership.

An *architecture description* is a formal description of an information system, organized in a way that supports reasoning about the structural properties of the system. It defines the components or building blocks that make up the overall information system, and provides a plan from which products can be procured, and systems developed, that will work together to implement the overall system. It thus enables you to manage your overall IT investment in a way that meets the needs of your business.

An *architecture framework* is a tool which can be used for developing a broad range of different architectures. It should describe a method for designing an information system in terms of a set of building blocks, and for showing how the building blocks fit together. It should contain a set of tools and provide a common vocabulary. It should also include a list of recommended standards and compliant products that can be used to implement the building blocks.

2.3 ArchiMate and TOGAF

TOGAF is an architecture framework – a set of methods and tools for developing a broad range of different IT architectures. It enables IT users to design, evaluate, and build the right architecture for their organization, and reduces the costs of planning, designing, and implementing architectures based on open systems solutions.

The key to TOGAF is the Architecture Development Method (ADM) – a reliable, proven method for developing an IT enterprise architecture that meets the needs of your business. The TOGAF framework considers an overall enterprise architecture as composed of a set of closely inter-related architectures: Business Architecture, Information Systems Architecture (comprising Data Architecture and Application Architecture), and Technology (IT) Architecture. The ADM consists of a stepwise cyclic iterative approach for the development of the overall enterprise architecture.

The ArchiMate language, as described in this Technical Standard, complements TOGAF in that it provides a vendor-independent set of concepts, including a graphical representation, that helps to create a consistent, integrated model "below the waterline", which can be depicted in the form of TOGAF's views.

The structure of the ArchiMate language neatly corresponds with the three main architectures as addressed in the TOGAF ADM. This is illustrated in Figure 1. This correspondence would suggest a fairly easy mapping between TOGAF's views and the ArchiMate viewpoints.

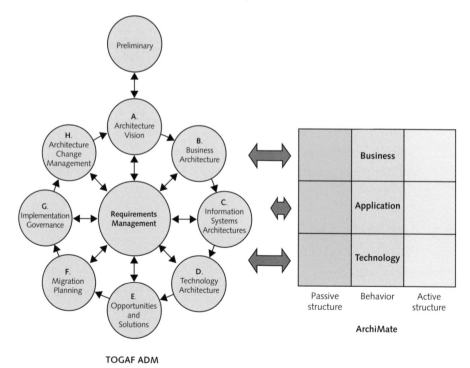

TOGAF ADM

Figure 1: Correspondence between ArchiMate and TOGAF

Some TOGAF views are not matched in ArchiMate, however. Partially, this is because TOGAF's scope is broader and in particular addresses more of the high-level strategic issues and the lower-level engineering aspects of system development, whereas ArchiMate is limited to the enterprise architecture level of abstraction and refers to other techniques both for strategies, principles, and objectives, and for more detailed, implementation-oriented aspects (however, Chapter 11 gives some suggestions for possible extensions of the ArchiMate language in these areas). Secondly, although some of the TOGAF views cannot easily be mapped onto ArchiMate viewpoints, the ArchiMate language and its analysis techniques do support the concepts addressed in these viewpoints. Conversely, ArchiMate viewpoints that deal with the relationships between architectural layers, such as the product and application usage viewpoints, are difficult to map onto TOGAF's structure, in which views are confined to a single architectural layer.

Although there is no one-to-one mapping between them, there is still a fair amount of correspondence between the ArchiMate viewpoints and the views that are defined in TOGAF. Although corresponding viewpoints from ArchiMate and TOGAF do not necessarily have identical coverage, we can see that many viewpoints from both methods address largely the same issues. TOGAF and ArchiMate can easily be used in conjunction and they appear to cover much of the same ground, be it with some differences in scope and approach.

Chapter 3

Language Structure

The unambiguous specification and description of enterprise architecture's components and especially of their relationships requires an architecture modeling language that addresses the issue of consistent alignment and facilitates a coherent modeling of enterprise architectures.

This chapter presents the construction of the ArchiMate architecture modeling language. The precise definition and illustration of its generic set of concepts follow in Chapters 4, 5, 6, 7, and 8. They provide a proper basis for visualization, analysis, tooling, and use of these concepts.

Sections 3.1 through 3.5 discuss some general ideas, principles, and assumptions underlying the development of the ArchiMate metamodel. Section 3.6 presents the ArchiMate framework, which will be used in the remainder of this document as a reference taxonomy scheme for architecture concepts, models, viewpoints, and views.

3.1 Design Approach

A key challenge in the development of a general metamodel for enterprise architecture is to strike a balance between the specificity of languages for individual architecture domains, and a very general set of architecture concepts, which reflects a view of systems as a mere set of inter-related entities. Figure 2 illustrates that concepts can be described at different levels of specialization.

At the base of the triangle we find the metamodels of the architecture modeling concepts used by specific organizations, as well as a variety of existing modeling languages and standards; UML is an example of a language in this category. At the top of the triangle we find the "most general" metamodel for system architectures, essentially a metamodel that merely comprises notions such as "object", "component", and "relation".

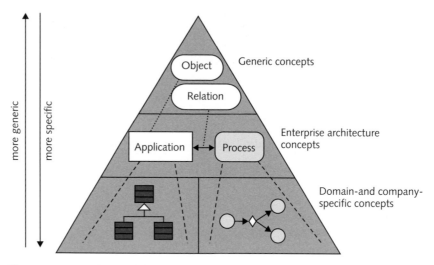

more generic

more specific

Figure 2: Metamodels at Different Levels of Specificity

The design of the ArchiMate language started from a set of relatively generic concepts (higher up in the pyramid). These were then specialized towards application at different architectural layers, as will be explained below.

The most important design restriction on the language is that it has been explicitly designed to be as small as possible, but still usable for most enterprise architecture modeling tasks. Many other languages, such as UML 2.0, try to accommodate all needs of all possible users. In the interest of simplicity of learning and use, ArchiMate has been limited to the concepts that suffice for modeling the proverbial 80% of practical cases.

3.2 Core Concepts

The language consists of *active structure* elements, *behavioral* elements and *passive structure* elements. The active structure elements are the business actors, application components and devices that display actual behavior, i.e., the 'subjects' of activity (right side of the Figure 3). Then there is the behavioral or dynamic aspect (center of Figure 3). The active structure concepts are assigned to behavioral concepts, to show who or what performs the behavior.

The passive structure elements are the objects on which behavior is performed. In the domain of information-intensive organizations, which is the main focus of the language, these are usually information or data objects,

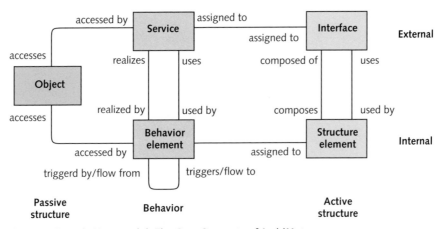

Figure 3: Generic Metamodel: The Core Concepts of ArchiMate

but they may also be used to represent physical objects. These three aspects – active structure, behavior, and passive structure – have been inspired by natural language, where a sentence has a subject (active structure), a verb (behavior), and an object (passive structure).

Second, we make a distinction between an external view and an internal view on systems. When looking at the behavioral aspect, these views reflect the principles of service orientation. The service concept represents a unit of essential functionality that a system exposes to its environment, and it provides a certain value (monetary or otherwise), which thus provides the motivation for the service's existence. For the external users, only this external functionality and value, together with non-functional aspects such as the quality of service, costs, etc., are relevant. These can be specified in a contract or Service Level Agreement (SLA). Services are accessible through interfaces, which constitute the external view on the active structural aspect.

3.3 Collaboration and Interaction

Going one level deeper in the structure of the language, we distinguish between behavior that is performed by a *single* structure element (e.g., actor, role component, etc.), or collective behavior (interaction) that is performed by a collaboration of multiple structure elements.

A collaboration is a (temporary) grouping (or aggregation) of two or more structure elements, working together to perform some collective behavior. This collective behavior can be modeled as an interaction.

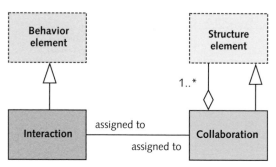

Figure 4: Collaboration and Interaction

3.4 Relationships

Next to the core concepts outlined above, ArchiMate contains a core set of relationships. Several of these relationships have been adopted from corresponding relationship concepts that occur in existing standards; e.g., relationships such as composition, aggregation, association, and specialization are taken from UML 2.0, while triggering is used in many business process modeling languages.

Note: For the sake of readability, the metamodel figures in the next sections do not show all possible relationships in the language. Refer to Section 8.5 on additional derived relationships. Furthermore, aggregation and composition relationships are always permitted between two elements that have the same type.

3.5 Layering

The ArchiMate language defines three main layers (depicted with different colors in the examples in the next chapters), based on specializations of the core concepts described in Sections 3.2 and 3.3:

1. The *Business Layer* offers products and services to external customers, which are realized in the organization by business processes performed by business actors.
2. The *Application Layer* supports the business layer with application services which are realized by (software) applications.
3. The *Technology Layer* offers infrastructure services (e.g., processing, storage, and communication services) needed to run applications, realized by computer and communication hardware and system software.

The general structure of models within the different layers is similar. The same types of concepts and relations are used, although their exact nature and granularity differ. In the next chapters, we will specialize these concepts to obtain more concrete concepts, which are specific for a certain layer. Figure 3 shows the central structure that is found in each layer.

In line with service orientation, the most important relation between layers is formed by "used by" relations, which show how the higher layers make use of the services of lower layers. (Note, however, that services may not only be used by elements in a higher layer, but also by elements in the same layer, as is shown in Figure 3.) A second type of link is formed by realization relationships: elements in lower layers may realize comparable elements in higher layers; e.g., a "data object" (Application layer) may realize a "business object" (Business layer); or an "artifact" (Technology layer) may realize either a "data object" or an "application component" (Application layer).

3.6 The ArchiMate Framework

The aspects and layers identified in the previous sections can be organized as a framework of nine "cells", as illustrated in Figure 5. The cells in this framework are a subset of the cells in, for example, the Zachman framework [5], [9]. Often used architectural domains can be projected into this framework; Figure 5 shows an example of this.

It is important to realize that the classification of concepts based on conceptual domains, or based on aspects and layers, is only a global one. It is impossible to define a strict boundary between the aspects and layers, because concepts that link the different aspects and layers play a central role in a coherent architectural description. For example, running somewhat ahead of the later conceptual discussions, (business) functions and (business) roles serve as intermediary concepts between "purely behavioral" concepts and "purely structural" concepts.

Besides the core aspects shown in Figure 5 (passive structure, behavior, and active structure), which are mainly operational in nature, there are a number of other important aspects, some of which may cross several (or all) conceptual domains; for example:
- Goals
- Security

- Governance
- Costs
- Performance
- Timing
- Planning and evolution

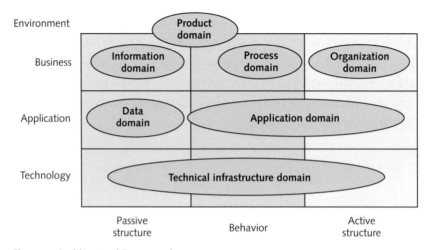

Figure 5: Architectural Framework

The aspects may be added to the models by means of additional concepts, relationships, or attributes. Also, it may be useful to add concepts or attributes related to the design process rather than to the system or organization that is to be described or designed. Examples of such concepts or attributes are requirements and design decisions. These aspects may be addressed in future extensions of the language (see Chapter 1 for a more thorough discussion of this).

Chapter 4

Business Layer

4.1 Business Layer Metamodel

Figure 6 shows the metamodel of business layer concepts. The metamodel follows the structure of the generic metamodel introduced in the previous chapter. However, this layer also includes a number of additional informational concepts which are relevant in the business domain: a product and associated contract, the meaning of business objects, and the value of products of business services.

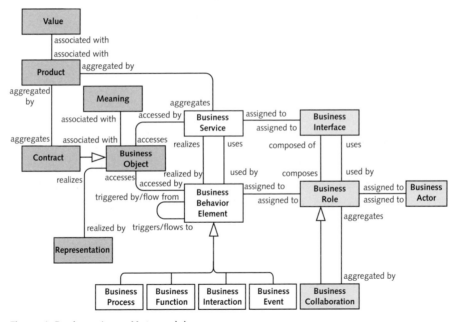

Figure 6: Business Layer Metamodel

Note: This figure does not show all permitted relationships: every element in the language can have composition and aggregation relations with elements of the same type; furthermore, there are indirect relationships that can be derived, as explained in Section 8.5.

4.2 Structural Concepts

The structure aspect at the business layer refers to the static structure of an organization, in terms of the entities that make up the organization and their relationships.

Two types of entities are distinguished:
- The *active entities* that are the subjects (e.g., business actors or business roles) that perform behavior such as business processes or functions (capabilities). Business actors may be individual persons (e.g., customers or employees), but also groups of people (organization units) and resources that have a permanent (or at least long-term) status within the organizations. Typical examples of the latter are a department and a business unit.
- The *passive entities* (business objects) that are manipulated by behavior such as business processes or functions. The passive entities represent the important concepts in which the business thinks about a domain.

Architectural descriptions focus on structure, which means that the inter-relationships of entities within an organization play an important role. To make this explicit, the concept of business collaboration has been introduced. Business collaborations have been inspired by collaborations as defined in the UML 2.0 standard [8], [12], although the UML collaborations apply to components in the application layer. Also, the ArchiMate business collaboration concept has a strong resemblance to the "community" concept as defined in the RM-ODP Enterprise Language [6], as well as to the "interaction point" concept, defined in Amber [13] as the place where interactions occur.

The concept of business interfaces is introduced to explicitly model the (logical or physical) locations or channels where the services that a role offers to the environment can be accessed. The same service may be offered on a number of different interfaces; e.g., by mail, by telephone, or through the Internet. In contrast to application modeling, it is uncommon in current business layer modeling approaches to recognize the business interface concept.

4.2.1 Business Actor

> A business actor is defined as an organizational entity capable of (actively) performing behavior.

A business actor performs the behavior assigned to (one or more) business roles. Examples of business actors are humans, departments, and business units. A business actor may be assigned to one or more business roles. The name of a business actor should preferably be a noun.

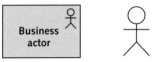

Figure 7: Business Actor Notation

Example

The model below illustrates the use of business actors. The company ArchiSurance is modeled as a business actor that is composed of two departments. The Travel insurance seller role is assigned to the travel department. In this role, the travel department performs the Take out insurance process, which offers a service that is accessible via the business interface assigned to this role.

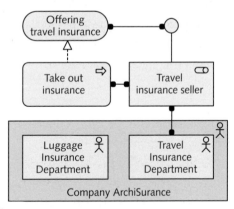

Example 1: Business Actor

4.2.2 Business Role

> A business role is defined as a named specific behavior of a business actor participating in a particular context.

Business processes or business functions are assigned to a single business role with certain responsibilities or skills. A business actor that is assigned to a business role ultimately performs the corresponding behavior. In addition to the relation of a business role with behavior, a business role is also useful in a (structural) organizational sense; for instance, in the division of labor within an organization.

A business role may be assigned to one or more business processes or business functions, while a business actor may be assigned to a business role. A business interface or an application interface may be used by a business role, while a business interface may be part of a business role (through a composition relation, which is not shown explicitly in the interface notation). The name of a business role should preferably be a noun.

Figure 8: Business Role Notation

Example

In the model below, two business roles (Luggage insurance seller and Travel insurance seller) are involved in a collaboration that results in a Combined insurance selling service. The left hand illustrates the delivery of a Luggage insurance selling service via a business interface. The right hand shows how a business process, Take out insurance, is assigned to the Travel insurance seller and realizes the Travel insurance selling service.

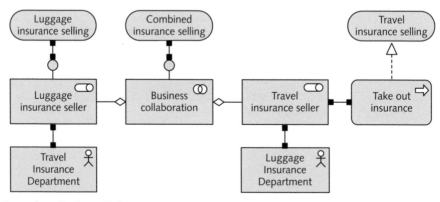

Example 2: Business Role

4.2.3 Business Collaboration

> Business collaboration is defined as a (temporary) configuration of two or more
> business roles resulting in specific collective behavior in a particular context.

A business process or function may be interpreted as the internal behavior
assigned to a single business role. In some cases behavior is the collective
effort of more than one business role; in fact a collaboration of two or
more business roles results in collective behavior which may be more than
simply the sum of the behavior of the separate roles. Business collaborations
represent this collective effort. Business interactions are used to describe
the internal behavior that takes place within business collaboration.
A collaboration is a (possibly temporary) collective of roles within an
organization which perform collaborative behavior (interactions). Unlike a
department, which may also group roles, a business collaboration does not
have an official (permanent) status within the organization; it is specifically
aimed at a specific interaction or set of interactions between roles. However,
a business collaboration can be regarded as a kind of "virtual role", hence its
designation as a specialization of role. It is especially useful in modeling B2B
interactions between different organizations.

A business collaboration may be composed of a number of business roles,
and may be assigned to one or more business interactions. A business
interface or an application interface may be used by a business collaboration,
while a business collaboration may have business interfaces (through
composition). The name of a business collaboration should preferably be a
noun. It is also rather common to leave a business collaboration unnamed.

Figure 9: Business Collaboration Notation

Example

The model in the model below illustrates a possible use of the collaboration concept. In this example, selling an insurance product involves the Sales department and a department specialized in that particular type of insurance. The example also shows that one role, in this case the Sales department, can participate in more than one collaboration.

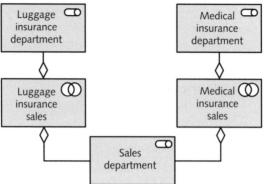

Example 3: Business Collaboration

4.2.4 Business Interface

A business interface declares how a business role can connect with its environment.

A business interface specifies how the functionality of a business role can be used by other business roles (provided interface), or which functionality the business roles requires from its environment (required interface). A business interface exposes a business service to the environment. The same business service may be exposed through different interfaces.

A business interface may be part of a business role through a composition relation, which is not shown in the standard notation, and a business interface may be used by a business role. A business interface may be assigned to one or more business services, which means that these services are exposed by the interface. The name of a business interface should preferably be a noun.

Figure 10: Business Interface Notation

Example

In the model below, the business services provided by the Luggage insurance seller and its collaboration with the Medical insurance seller are exposed by means of a web form and call center business interface, respectively.

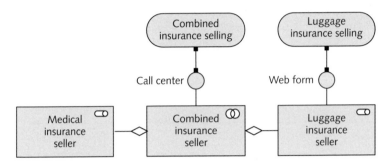

Example 4: Business Interface

4.2.5 Business Object

A business object is defined as a unit of information that has relevance from a business perspective.

Business objects represent the important "informational" or "conceptual" elements in which the business thinks about a domain. Generally, a business object is used to model an object type (cf. a UML class), of which several instances may exist within the organization. A wide variety of types of business objects can be defined. Business objects are passive in the sense that they do not trigger or perform processes.

A business object may be accessed (e.g., created, read, written) by a business process, function, a business interaction, a business event, or a business service. A business object may have association, specialization, aggregation, or composition relationships with other business objects. A business object may be realized by a representation or by a data object (or both). The name of a business object should preferably be a noun.

Figure 11: Business Object Notation

Example

The model below shows a business object Invoice, which aggregates (multiple) business objects Invoice line. Two possible realizations of this business object exist: an Electronic invoice (data object) and a Paper invoice (representation). The business process Create invoice creates the invoice and the invoice lines, while the business process Send invoice accesses the business object Invoice.

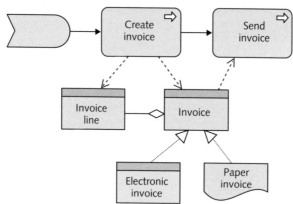

Example 5: Business Object

4.3 Behavioral Concepts

Based on service orientation, a crucial design decision for the behavioral part of our metamodel is the distinction between "external" and "internal" behavior of an organization.

The externally visible behavior is modeled by the concept *business service*. A business service represents a coherent piece of functionality that offers added value to the environment, independent of the way this functionality is realized internally. A distinction can be made between "external" business services, offered to external customers, and "internal" business services, offering supporting functionality to processes or functions within the organization.

Several types of internal behavior elements that can realize a service are distinguished. Although the distinction between the two is not always sharp, it is often useful to distinguish a *process view* and a *function view* on behavior; two concepts associated with these views, *business process* and *business function*, are defined. Both concepts can be used to group more detailed business processes/functions, but based on different grouping criteria. A *business process* represents a workflow or value stream consisting of smaller processes/functions, with one or more clear starting points and leading to some result. It is sometimes described as "customer to customer", where this customer may also be an internal customer, in the case of sub-processes within an organization. The goal of such a business process is to "satisfy or delight the customer" [14]. A *business function* offers functionality that may be useful for one or more business processes. It groups behavior based on, for example, required skills, capabilities, resources, (application) support, etc. Other methods sometimes call this a *business capability*. Typically, the business processes of an organization are defined based on the *products* and *services* that the organization offers, while the business functions are the basis for, for example, the assignment of resources to tasks and the application support.

A *business interaction* is a unit of behavior similar to a business process or function, but which is performed in a collaboration of two or more roles within the organization. Unlike the interaction concept in Amber [13], which is an *atomic* unit of collaborative behavior, our business interaction can be decomposed into smaller interactions. Although interactions are external behavior from the perspective of the roles participating in the collaboration, the behavior is internal to the collaboration as a whole. Similar to processes or functions, the result of a business interaction can be made available to the environment through a business service.

A *business event* is something that happens (externally) and may influence business processes, functions, or interactions. The "business event" concept is similar to the "trigger" concept in Amber [13] and the "initial state" and "final state" concepts as used in, for example, UML activity diagrams. However, our business event is more generally applicable in the sense that it can also be used to model other types of events, in addition to triggers.

4.3.1 Business Process

> A business process is defined as a unit of internal behavior or collection of causally-related units of internal behavior intended to produce a defined set of products and services.

A business process describes the internal behavior performed by a business role that is required to produce a set of products and services. For a consumer the products and services are relevant and the required behavior is merely a black box, hence the designation "internal".

In comparison to a business interaction, in which more than two business roles are (interactively) involved, only one business role is involved with a business process. However, a (complex) business process may consist of sub-processes assigned to different business roles.

There is a potential many-to-many relation between business processes and business functions. Informally speaking, processes describe some kind of "flow" of activities, whereas functions group activities according to required skills, knowledge, resources, etc.

A business process may be triggered by, or trigger, any other business behavior element (e.g., business event, business process, business function, or business interaction). A business process may access business objects. A business process may realize one or more business services and may use (internal) business services or application services. A business role or an application component may be assigned to a business process to perform this process manually or automated, respectively. The name of a business process should preferably be a verb in the simple present tense; e.g., "handle claim".

Figure 12: Business Process Notation

Example

The model below illustrates the use of business processes and its relation with other concepts. The Take out insurance process is composed of three sub-processes. For clarity, the sub-processes are drawn in the overall process (structuring). Each sub-process triggers the next sub-process. The event Request for Insurance triggers the first sub-process. A particular role, in this case an insurance seller, is assigned to perform the required work. The process itself realizes an Insurance selling service. The Receive request sub-process uses the business object Customer info. Also, during the take out process, the Process request sub-process makes use of an application service Transaction entry.

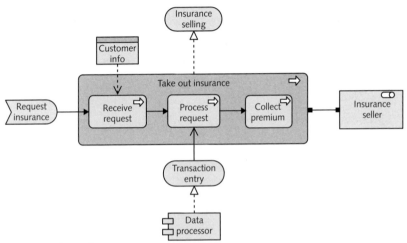

Example 6: Business Process

4.3.2 Business Function

A business function is defined as a unit of internal behavior that groups behavior according to, for example, required skills, knowledge, resources, etc., and is performed by a single role within the organization.

A business function describes internal behavior performed by a business role that is required to produce a set of products and services. For a consumer, the products and services are relevant and the required behavior is merely a black box, hence the designation "internal".

There is a potential many-to-many relation between business processes and business functions. Informally speaking, processes describe some kind of "flow" of activities, whereas functions group activities according to required skills, knowledge, resources etc. Complex processes in general involve activities that offer various functions. In this sense a business process forms a string of business functions. In general, a business function delivers added value from a business point of view. Organizational units or applications may coincide with business functions due to their specific grouping of business activities.

A business function may be triggered by, or trigger, any other business behavior element (business event, business process, business function, or business interaction). A business function may access business objects. A business function may realize one or more business services and may use (internal) business services or application services. A business role or an application component may be assigned to a business function. The name of a business function should preferably be a verb ending with "-ing"; e.g., "claims processing".

Figure 13: Business Function Notation

Example

The model below illustrates the use of business functions, as well as the relation between business functions and business processes. The three business functions group a number of business sub-processes. The business process, initiated by a business event, involves sub-processes from different business functions. The Insurer role is assigned to each of the business functions. Moreover, business functions may access business objects; in this case, the Customer contact function uses or manipulates the Customer info object. Also, the Financial settlement function makes use of a Billing application service and realizes a Collecting premium business service.

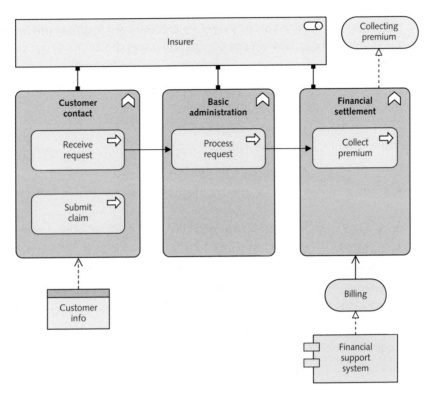

Example 7: Business Function

4.3.3 Business Interaction

> Business interaction is defined as a unit of behavior performed as a collaboration of two or more business roles.

A business interaction is similar to a business process/function, but while a process/function may be performed by a single role, an interaction is performed by multiple roles in collaboration.

A business interaction may be triggered by, or trigger, any other business behavior element (business event, business process, business function, or business interaction). A business interaction may access business objects. A business interaction may realize one or more business services and may use (internal) business services or application services. A business collaboration or an application collaboration may be assigned to a business interaction. The name of a business interaction should preferably be a verb in the simple present tense.

Figure 14: Business Interaction Notation

Example

In the model below, a business interaction is triggered by a request. The business interaction Take out combined insurance is performed as collaboration between the travel and luggage insurance seller. The business interaction needs the Policy info business object, and realizes the (external) business service Combined insurance selling. As part of the business interaction, the Prepare travel policy and Prepare luggage policy are triggered. The Travel insurance seller and Luggage insurance seller perform these processes separately.

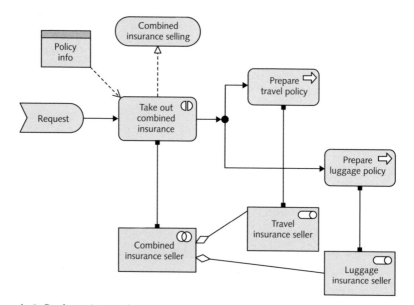

Example 8: Business Interaction

4.3.4 Business Event

> A business event is defined as something that happens (internally or externally) and influences behavior (business process, business function, business interaction).

Business processes and other business behavior may be triggered or interrupted by a business event. Also, business processes may raise events that trigger other business processes, functions, or interactions. A business event is most commonly used to model something that triggers behavior, but other types of events are also conceivable; e.g., an event that interrupts a process. Unlike business processes, functions, and interactions, a business event is instantaneous: it does not have duration. Events may originate from the environment of the organization (e.g., from a customer), but also internal events may occur generated by, for example, other processes within the organization.

A business event may trigger or be triggered (raised) by a business process, business function, or business interaction. A business event may access a business object and may be composed of other business events. The name of a business event should preferably be a verb in the perfect tense; e.g., "claim received".

Figure 15: Business Event Notation

Example

In the model below, the Request insurance event triggers the Take out insurance process. A business object containing the Customer info accompanies the request. In order to persuade the customer to purchase more insurance products, a triggering event is raised in the Receive request process. This triggers the Send product portfolio to customer process.

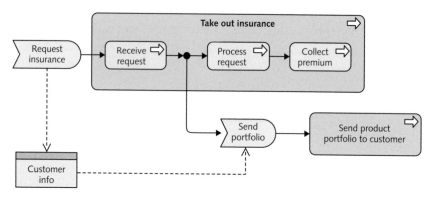

Example 9: Business Event

4.3.5 Business Service

> A business service is defined as the externally visible ("logical") functionality,
> which is meaningful to the environment and is realized by business behavior
> (business process, business function, or business interaction).

A business service exposes the functionality of business roles or collaborations to their environment. This functionality is accessed through one or more business interfaces. A business service is realized by one or more business processes, business functions, or business interactions that are performed by the business roles or business collaborations, respectively. It may access business objects.

A business service should provide a unit of functionality that is meaningful from the point of view of the environment. It has a purpose, which states this utility. The environment includes the (behavior of) users from outside as well as inside the organization.

A business service is associated with a value. A business service may be used by a business process, business function, or business interaction. A business process, business function, or business interaction may realize a business service. A business interface or application interface may be assigned to a business service. A business service may access business objects. The name of a business service should preferably be a verb ending with "-ing"; e.g., "transaction processing". Also, a name explicitly containing the word "service" may be used.

Figure 16: Business Service Notation

Example

In the model below, external and internal business services are distinguished. The Basic administration function acts as a shared service center. The take out business processes corresponding with the travel and luggage insurance use the (internal) business services that are provided by the Basic administration function. Both business processes realize an (external) business service. The insurance selling service is accessible via a business interface (e.g., web form) that is used by the insurer. Each business service should be of value to its environment, which may or may not be explicitly modeled. The value of the Travel insurance selling service to an external customer is that the customer is insured.

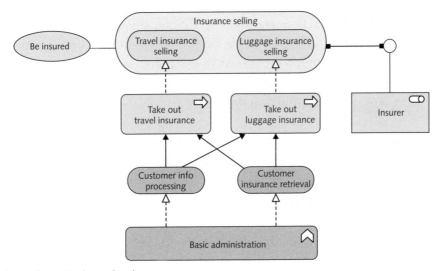

Example 10: Business Service

4.4 Informational Concepts

In contrast to the structural and behavioral concepts, which are mainly concerned with the operational perspective on an enterprise, the informational concepts focus on what we could call the "intentional" perspective. They provide a way to link the operational side of an organization to the business goals, and to the products that an organization offers to its customers. We also classify the product concept itself, together with the related contract concept, as informational concepts.

Information is fundamentally related to communication. Information always serves a particular purpose, which is tightly connected to some communicational goal. As communication always involves a static part (the "message") and a dynamic part (the communication action itself), the communicational goals may have a link to both our "meaning" concept and our "value" concept. Also, in speech act-based approaches to business modeling, such as DEMO [10], the communicational aspect plays a central role in the context of business transactions.

A *representation* is the perceptible form of the information carried by a business object, such as a document. As such, it can be seen as the realization of the associated business object. If relevant, representations can be classified in various ways; for example, in terms of medium (e.g., electronic, paper, audio) or format (e.g., HTML, PDF, plain text, bar chart).

A *meaning* is the contribution of the representation of a business object to the knowledge or expertise of some actor, given a particular context. In other words, meaning represents the informative value of a business object for a user of such an object. It is through a certain interpretation of a representation of the object that meaning is being offered to a certain user or to a certain category of users. A meaning can very well be a reformulation or transformation of parts of the object representation in such a way that the role of the meaning is immediately clear within the user's world, but essentially lies in interpretation by individuals, in context.

For the complete description of a meaning, the following two elements are needed, in addition to the representations (and, indirectly, business objects) with which the meaning is associated:
- Some sort of *meaning description*: A meaning description is not equal to the representation causing the meaning: it is a specialized description

that aims to clarify or stipulate a meaning. Natural language may be used for this, but also formal languages or diagrams. Typical examples of meaning descriptions are definitions, ontologies, paraphrases, subject descriptions, and tables of content. Meaning descriptions may draw from or refer to additional meaning description sources; for example, dictionaries. Importantly, meaning descriptions *do not necessarily have to describe meaning in detail*. The level of detail depends on the types of analysis required. It is quite possible that a very rough meaning description is *good enough* to capture at architecture level the sort of interpretations a business object conveys. Detailed meaning description can only in a limited number of cases be made very precise; in most cases, interpretation depends on the general language and knowledge of specific actors, which normally remains largely implicit.

- A description of the *context(s)* in which the meaning is conveyed: A context description covers the situation in which the interpretation takes place. The most important elements of such a context are the *actors sending and receiving the business object*, the *time and place* of communication and the *environment in which this happens*. Often, a context can be briefly described in terms of some business domain.

We see a (financial or information) *product* as of a collection of services, together with a contract that specifies the characteristics, rights, and requirements associated with the product. This "package" is offered as a whole to (internal or external) customers.

We define a *contract* as a formal or informal specification of agreement that specifies the rights and obligations associated with a product. The *value* of a product or service is that which makes some party appreciate it, possibly in relation to providing it, but more typically to acquiring it.

4.4.1 Representation

> Representation is defined as the perceptible form of the information carried by a business object.

Representations (for example, messages or documents) are the perceptible carriers of information that are related to business objects. If relevant, representations can be classified in various ways; for example, in terms of medium (electronic, paper, audio, etc.) or format (HTML, ASCII, PFD, RTF, etc.). A single business object can have a number of different representations, but a representation always belongs to one specific business object.

A representation may realize one or more business objects. A meaning can be associated with a representation that carries this meaning. The name of a representation is preferably a noun.

Figure 17: Representation Notation

Example
The model below shows the business object Request for insurance, which is realized (represented) by a (physical) request form. The Invoice business object is realized (represented) by a paper bill.

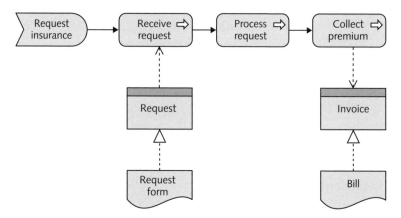

Example 11: Representation

4.4.2 Meaning

Meaning is defined as the knowledge or expertise present in the representation of a business object, given a particular context.

A meaning is the representation-related counterpart of a value: it represents the functionality of a representation (for example, a document, message; the representations related to a business object). It is a description that expresses the *intent* of a representation; i.e., how it informs the *external user*.

It is possible that different users view the informative functionality of a representation differently. For example, what may be a "registration confirmation" for a client could be a "client mutation" for a CRM department (assuming for the sake of argument that it is modeled as an external user). Also, various different representations may carry essentially the same meaning. For example, various different documents (a web document, a filled-in paper form, a "client contact" report from the call center) may essentially carry the same meaning.

A meaning can be associated with a representation that carries this meaning. The name of a meaning should preferably be a noun or noun phrase.

Figure 18: Meaning Notation

Example

The model below shows an Insurance policy document that is the representation of an Insurance policy, which is a business object. The meaning related to this document is the Insurance policy notification, which consists of a Policy explanation, an Insurance registration, and a Coverage description.

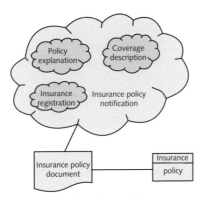

Example 12: Meaning

4.4.3 Value

> Value is defined as that which makes some party appreciate a service or product, possibly in relation to providing it, but more typically to acquiring it.

Value may apply to what a party gets by selling or making available some product or service, or it may apply to what a party gets by buying or obtaining access to it. Value is often expressed in terms of money, but it has long since been recognized that non-monetary value is also essential to business; for example, practical/functional value (including the *right* to use a service), and the value of information or knowledge. Though value can hold internally for some system or organizational unit, it is most typically applied to *external* appreciation of goods, services, information, knowledge, or money, normally as part of some sort of customer-provider relationship.

A value can be associated with business services and, indirectly, with the products they are part of, and the roles or actors that use them. Although the name of a value can be expressed in many different ways (including amounts, objects), where the "functional" value of a service is concerned it is recommended to try and express it as an action or state that can be performed or reached as a result of the corresponding service being available.

Figure 19: Value Notation

> **Example**
>
> In the model below, the value Be Insured is the highest-level expression of what the service Provide Insurance enables the client to do; three "sub-values" are distinguished that are part of what Be Insured amounts to.

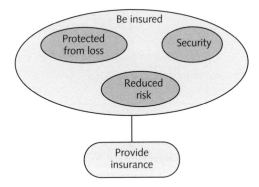

Example 13: Value

4.4.4 Product

> A product is defined as a coherent collection of services, accompanied by a
> contract/set of agreements, which is offered as a whole to (internal or external)
> customers.

A (financial or information) product consists of a collection of services,
and a contract that specifies the characteristics, rights, and requirements
associated with the product. "Buying" a product gives the customer the right
to use the associated services. Generally, the product concept is used to
specify a product *type*. The number of product types in an organization is
typically relatively stable compared to, for example, the processes that realize
or support the products. "Buying" is usually one of the services associated
with a product, which results in a new instance of that product (belonging to
a specific customer). Similarly, there may be services to modify or destroy a
product.

A product may aggregate business services or application services,[1] as well as
a contract. A value may be associated with a product. The name of a product
is usually the name which is used in the communication with customers, or
possibly a more generic noun (e.g., "travel insurance").

---
1 The latter relation is defined in Chapter 7 on cross-layer dependencies.

Figure 20: Product Notation

Example

In the model below, a bank offers the product Telebanking account to its customers. Opening an account as well as application support (i.e., helpdesk and the like), are modeled as business services realized by the Customer relations department. As part of the product, the customer can make use of a banking service which offers application services realized by the Telebanking application, such as electronic Money transfer and requesting Account status.

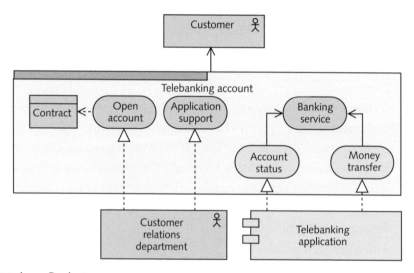

Example 14: Product

4.4.5 Contract

A contract is defined as a formal or informal specification of an agreement that specifies the rights and obligations associated with a product.

The contract concept may be used to model a contract in the legal sense, but also a more informal agreement associated with a product. It may also be or include a Service Level Agreement (SLA), describing an agreement about the functionality and quality of the services that are part of a product. A contract is a specialization of a business object.

The relationships that apply to a business object also apply to a contract. In addition, a contract may have an aggregation relationship with a product. The name of a contract is preferably a noun.

Figure 21: Contract Notation

Example

The model below shows a Telebanking contract associated with the product Telebanking account. The contract consists of two parts (subcontracts): the Service Conditions and a Service Level Agreement.

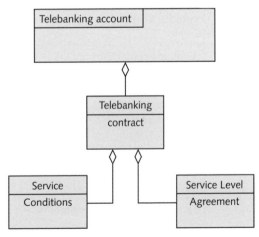

Example 15: Contract

4.5 Summary of Business Layer Concepts

Table 1 gives an overview of the concepts at the business layer, with their definitions.

Table 1: Business Layer Concepts

Concept	Description	Notation
Business actor	An organizational entity that is capable of performing behavior.	Business actor
Business role	A named specific behavior of a business actor participating in a particular context.	Business role
Business collaboration	A (temporary) configuration of two or more business roles resulting in specific collective behavior in a particular context.	Business collaboration
Business interface	Declares how a business role can connect with its environment.	Business interface
Business object	A unit of information that has relevance from a business perspective.	Business object
Business process	A unit of internal behavior or collection of causally related units of internal behavior intended to produce a defined set of products and services.	Business process
Business function	A unit of internal behavior that groups behavior according to, for example, required skills, knowledge, resources, etc., and is performed by a single role within the organization.	Business function
Business interaction	A unit of behavior performed as a collaboration of two or more business roles.	Business interaction
Business event	Something that happens (internally or externally) and influences behavior.	Business event
Business service	An externally visible unit of functionality, which is meaningful to the environment and is provided by a business role.	Business service
Representation	The perceptible form of the information carried by a business object.	Representation

Concept	Description	Notation
Meaning	The knowledge or expertise present in the representation of a business object, given a particular context.	Meaning
Value	That which makes some party appreciate a service or product, possibly in relation to providing it, but more typically to acquiring it.	Value
Product	A coherent collection of services, accompanied by a contract/set of agreements, which is offered as a whole to (internal or external) customers.	Product
Contract	A formal or informal specification of agreement that specifies the rights and obligations associated with a product.	Contract

Chapter 5

Application Layer

5.1 Application Layer Metamodel

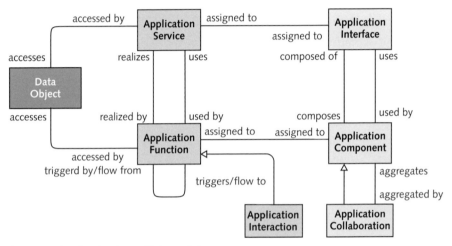

Figure 22: Application Layer Metamodel

Note: This figure does not show all permitted relationships: every element in the language can have composition and aggregation relations with elements of the same type; furthermore, there are indirect relationships that can be derived as explained in Section 8.5.

5.2 Structural Concepts

The main structural concept for the application layer is the *application component*. This concept is used to model any structural entity in the application layer: not just (re-usable) software components that can be part of one or more applications, but also complete software applications, sub-applications, or information systems. Although very similar to the UML 2.0 component, our component concept strictly models the structural aspect of an application: its behavior is modeled by an explicit relationship to the behavioral concepts.

Also in application architecture, the inter-relationships of components are an essential ingredient. Therefore, we also introduce the concept of *application collaboration* here, defined as a collective of application components which perform application interactions. The concept is very similar to the collaboration as defined in the UML 2.0 standard [8], [12].

In the purely structural sense, an *application interface* is the (logical) channel through which the services of a component can be accessed. In a broader sense (as used in, among others, the UML 2.0 definition), an application interface defines some elementary behavioral characteristics: it defines the set of operations and events that are provided by the component, or those that are required from the environment. Thus, it is used to describe the functionality of a component. A distinction may be made between a *provided interface* and a *required interface*. The application interface concept can be used to model both *application-to-application* interfaces, which offer internal application services, and *application-to business* interfaces (and/or *user interfaces*), which offer external application services.

Also at the application layer, we distinguish the passive counterpart of the component, which we call a *data object*. This concept is used in the same way as data objects (or object types) in well-known data modeling approaches, most notably the "class" concept in UML class diagrams. A data object can be seen as a representation of a business object, as a counterpart of the representation concept in the business layer.

5.2.1 Application Component

> An application component is defined as a modular, deployable, and replaceable part of a system that encapsulates its contents and exposes its functionality through a set of interfaces.

An application component is a self-contained unit of functionality. As such, it is independently deployable, re-usable, and replaceable. An application component performs one or more application functions. It encapsulates its contents: its functionality is only accessible through a set of application interfaces. Co-operating application components are connected via application collaborations.

An application component may be assigned to one or more application functions, business processes, or business functions. An application component has (is composed of) one or more application interfaces, which exposes its functionality. Application interfaces of other application components may be used by an application component. The name of an application component should preferably be a noun.

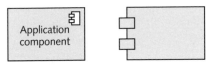

Figure 23: Application Component Notation

Example

In the model below, a financial application is depicted as an application component consisting of two collaborating subcomponents for accounting and billing.

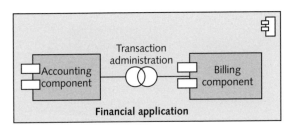

Example 16: Application Component

5.2.2 Application Collaboration

Application collaboration is defined as a (temporary) configuration of two or more components that co-operate to jointly perform application interactions.

An application collaboration specifies which components (have to) co-operate to perform some task. The collaborative behavior, including, for example, the communication pattern of these components, is modeled by an application interaction.

An application collaboration is a specialization of a component, and aggregates two or more (co-operating) application components. An application collaboration may be assigned to one or more application interactions or business interactions. An application interface may be used by an application collaboration, and an application collaboration may be composed of application interfaces. The name of an application collaboration should preferably be a noun.

Figure 24: Application Collaboration Notation

Example

In the model below, two components collaborate in transaction administration: an Accounting component and a Billing component. This collaboration performs the application interaction Administrate transactions.

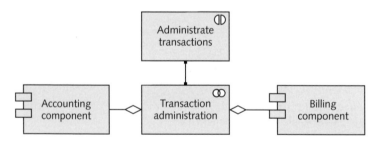

Example 17: Application Collaboration

5.2.3 Application Interface

An application interface declares how a component can connect with its environment.

An application interface specifies how the functionality of a component can be accessed by other components (provided interface), or which functionality the component requires from its environment (required interface). An application interface exposes an application service to the environment. The same application service may be exposed through different interfaces.

In a sense, an application interface specifies a kind of contract that a component realizing this interface must fulfill. This may include parameters, protocols used, pre- and post-conditions, and data formats.

An application interface may be part of an application component through composition (not shown in the standard notation), which means that these interfaces are provided or required by that component, and can be used by other application components. An application interface can be assigned to application services or business services, which means that the interface exposes these services to the environment. The name of an application interface should preferably be a noun.

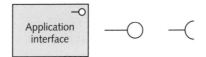

Figure 25: Application Interface Notation

Example

In the model below, an Accounting component is shown that provides an application interface for Transaction data exchange, and a Billing component that requires such an interface.

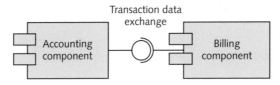

Example 18: Application Interface

5.2.4 Data Object

> A data object is defined as a coherent, self-contained piece of information suitable for automated processing.

An application function operates on a data object. A data object may be communicated via interactions and used or produced by application services. It should be a useful, self-contained piece of information with a clear meaning to the business, not just to the application level. Typical examples of data objects are a customer record, a client database, or an insurance claim.

A data object can be accessed by an application function, application interaction, or application service. A data object may realize a business object, and may be realized by an artifact. A data object may have association, specialization, aggregation, or composition relationships with other data objects. The name of a data object should preferably be a noun.

Figure 26: Data Object Notation

> **Example**
> In the model below, two application functions co-operate via an application service, in which a data object holding Transaction data is exchanged.

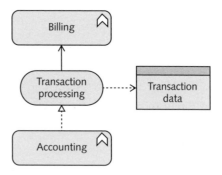

Example 19: Data Object

5.3 Behavioral Concepts

Behavior at the application layer can be described in a way that is very similar to business layer behavior. Also here, we make a distinction between the external behavior of application components in terms of *application services*, and the internal behavior of these components; i.e., application functions that realize these services.

An *application service* is an externally visible unit of functionality, provided by one or more components, exposed through well-defined interfaces, and meaningful to the environment. The service concept provides a way to explicitly describe the functionality that components share with each other and the functionality that they make available to the environment. The concept fits well within the current developments in the area of web services. The functionality that an interactive computer program provides through a user interface is also modeled using an application service, exposed by an application-to-business interface representing the user interface. Internal application services are exposed through an application-to-application interface.

An *application function* describes the internal behavior of a component needed to realize one or more application services. In analogy with the business layer, a separate "application flow" concept is conceivable as the counterpart of a business process. Note that the internal behavior of a component should in most cases not be modeled in too much detail in an architectural description, because for the description of this behavior we may soon be confronted with detailed design issues.

An *application interaction* is the behavior of a collaboration of two or more application components. The UML 2.0 standard [8], [12] also includes the interaction concept. An application component is external behavior from the perspective of each of the participating components, but the behavior is internal to the collaboration as a whole.

5.3.1 Application Function

An application function is defined as a representation of a coherent group of internal behavior of an application component.

An application function describes the internal behavior of a component; for the user of a component that performs an application function, this function is invisible. If its behavior is exposed externally, this is done through one or more services. An application function abstracts from the way it is implemented. Only the necessary behavior is specified.

An application function may realize application services. Application services of other application functions and infrastructure services may be used by an application function. An application function may access data objects. An application component may be assigned to an application function (which means that the application component performs the application function). The name of an application function should preferably be a verb ending with "-ing"; e.g., "accounting".

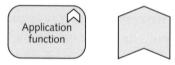

Figure 27: Application Function Notation

Example

In the model below, the functionality of a Financial application is modeled as an application function consisting of two sub-functions.

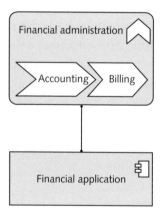

Example 20: Application Function

5.3.2 Application Interaction

> Application interaction is defined as a unit of behavior performed by a
> collaboration of two or more components.

An application interaction describes the externally visible behavior that is
performed by components that participate in an application collaboration.
This may, for example, include the communication pattern between these
components. An application interaction can also specify the externally visible
behavior needed to realize an application service.

An application collaboration may be assigned to an application interaction.
An application interaction may realize an application service. Application
services and infrastructure services may be used by an application
interaction. An application interaction may access data objects. The name of
an application interaction should preferably be a verb.

Figure 28: Application Interaction Notation

> **Example**
>
> In the model below, an Accounting component and a Billing component of a
> financial system co-operate to compose an *administrate transactions* interaction.
> This is modeled as an application interaction assigned to the collaboration
> between the two components.

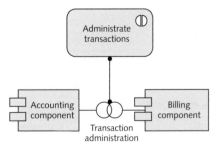

Example 21: Application Collaboration

5.3.3 Application Service

> An application service is defined as an externally visible unit of functionality, provided by one or more components, exposed through well-defined interfaces, and meaningful to the environment.

An application service exposes the functionality of components to their environment. This functionality is accessed through one or more application interfaces. An application service is realized by one or more application functions that are performed by the component. It may require, use, and produce data objects.

An application service should be meaningful from the point of view of the environment; it should provide a unit of functionality that is in itself useful to its users. It has a purpose, which states this utility to the environment. This means, for example, that if this environment includes business processes, application services should have business relevance.

A purpose may be associated with an application service. An application service may be used by business processes, business functions, business interactions, or application functions. An application function may realize an application service. An application interface may be assigned to an application service. An application service may access data objects. The name of an application service should preferably be a verb ending with "-ing"; e.g., "transaction processing". Also, a name explicitly containing the word "service" may be used.

Figure 29: Application Service Notation

> **Example**
> In the model below, a Transaction processing service is realized by the Accounting application function. This service is assigned to the Transaction data exchange interface and used by the Billing application function.

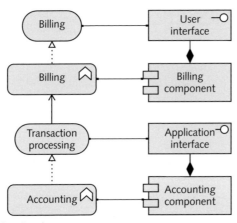

Example 22: Application Service

5.4 Summary of Application Layer Components

Table 2 gives an overview of the concepts at the application layer, with their definitions.

Table 2: Application Layer Concepts

Concept	Definition	Notation
Application component	A modular, deployable, and replaceable part of a system that encapsulates its contents and exposes its functionality through a set of interfaces.	
Application collaboration	An application collaboration defines a (temporary) configuration of two or more components that co-operate to jointly perform application interactions.	
Application interface	An application interface declares how a component can connect with its environment.	
Data object	A coherent, self-contained piece of information suitable for automated processing.	
Application function	A coherent group of internal behavior of a component.	
Application interaction	A unit of behavior jointly performed by two or more collaborating components.	

Concept	Definition	Notation
Application service	An externally visible unit of functionality, provided by one or more components, exposed through well-defined interfaces, and meaningful to the environment.	Application service

Chapter 6

Technology Layer

6.1 Technology Layer Metamodel

Figure 30 gives an overview of the technology layer concepts and their relationships. Many of the concepts have been inspired by the UML 2.0 standard [8], [12], as this is the dominant language and the *de facto* standard for describing software applications. Whenever applicable, we draw inspiration from the analogy with the business and application layers.

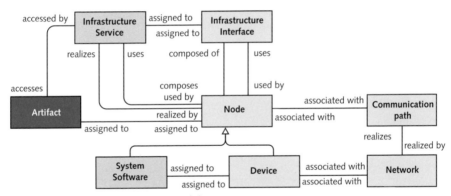

Figure 30: Technology Layer Metamodel

Note: This figure does not show all permitted relationships: every element in the language can have composition and aggregation relations with elements of the same type; furthermore, there are indirect relationships that can be derived as explained in Section 8.5.

6.2 Structural Concepts

The main structural concept for the technology layer is the *node*. This concept is used to model structural entities in this layer. It is identical to the node concept of UML 2.0. It strictly models the structural aspect of a system: its behavior is modeled by an explicit relationship to the behavioral concepts.

An *infrastructure interface* is the (logical) location where the infrastructure services offered by a node can be accessed by other nodes or by application components from the application layer.

Nodes come in two flavors: *device* and *system software*, both taken from UML 2.0. A *device* models a physical computational resource, upon which artifacts may be deployed for execution. *System software* is classified as a behavioral concept, since it defines what a device "does". Typically, a node will consist of a number of sub-nodes; for example, a device such as a server and system software to model the operating system.

The inter-relationships of components in the technology layer are mainly formed by the communication infrastructure. The *communication path* models the relation between two or more nodes, through which these nodes can exchange information. The physical realization of a communication path is a modeled with a *network*; i.e., a physical communication medium between two or more devices (or other networks).

6.2.1 Node

A node is defined as a computational resource upon which artifacts may be deployed for execution.

Nodes are active processing elements that execute and process artifacts, which are the representation of components and data objects. Nodes are, for example, used to model application servers, database servers, or client workstations. They can consist of sub-nodes representing physical devices and execution environments for artifacts.

Nodes can be interconnected by communication paths. Artifacts can be assigned to (i.e., deployed on) nodes.

The name of a node should preferably be a noun. A node can consist of sub-nodes.

Artifacts deployed on a node may either be drawn inside the node or connected to it with an assignment relation.

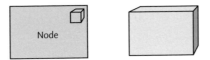

Figure 31: Node Notation

Example

In the model below, we see an Application Server node, which consists of a Sun Blade device and a JBoss J2EE Server application.

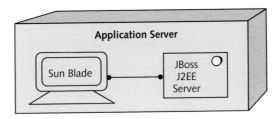

Example 23: Node

6.2.2 Device

A device is defined as a physical computational resource upon which artifacts may be deployed for execution.

A device is a specialization of a node that represents a physical resource with processing capability. It is typically used to model hardware systems such as mainframes, PCs, or routers. Usually, they are part of a node together with system software. Devices may be composite; i.e., consist of sub-devices.

Devices can be interconnected by networks. Artifacts can be assigned to (i.e., deployed on) devices. System software can be assigned to a device. A node can contain one or more devices.

The name of a device should preferably be a noun referring to the type of hardware; e.g., "IBM System z mainframe".

A device can consist of sub-devices.

Different icons may be used to distinguish between different types of devices; e.g. mainframes and PCs.

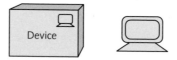

Figure 32: Device Notation

Example

In the model below, we see a device IBM Systems z to which DB2 system software is assigned.

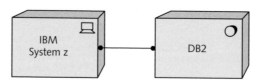

Example 24: Device

6.2.3 Infrastructure Interface

An infrastructure interface is defined as a point of access where the functionality offered by a node can be accessed by other nodes and application components.

An infrastructure interface specifies how the infrastructure services of a node can be accessed by other nodes (provided interface), or which functionality the node requires from its environment (required interface). An infrastructure interface exposes an infrastructure service to the environment. The same service may be exposed through different interfaces.

In a sense, an infrastructure interface specifies a kind of contract that a component realizing this interface must fulfill. This may include, for example, parameters, protocols used, pre- and post-conditions, and data formats.

An infrastructure interface may be part of a node through composition (not shown in the standard notation), which means that these interfaces are provided or required by that node, and can be used by other nodes. An infrastructure service can be assigned to an infrastructure interface, which exposes the service to the environment.

The name of an infrastructure interface should preferably be a noun.

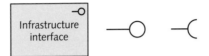

Figure 33: Infrastructure Interface Notations

Example

In the model below, we see a Sybase Open Client infrastructure interface exposed, which is part of the Sybase system software.

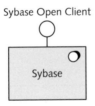

Example 25: Infrastructure Interface

6.2.4 Network

A network is defined as a physical communication medium between two or more devices.

A network represents the physical communication infrastructure. This may comprise one or more fixed or wireless network links. The most basic network is a single link between two devices. A network has properties such as bandwidth and latency. It embodies the physical realization of the logical communication paths between nodes.

A network connects two or more devices. A network realizes one or more communication paths.

A network can consist of sub-networks.

Figure 34: Network Notation, as Connection and as Box

Example

In the model below, a 100 Mb/s LAN network connects a mainframe and PC device.

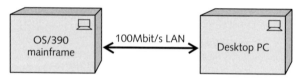

Example 26: Network

6.2.5 Communication Path

A communication path is defined as a link between two or more nodes, through which these nodes can exchange information.

A communication path is used to model the logical communication relations between nodes. It is realized by one or more networks, which represent the physical communication links. The communication properties (e.g., bandwidth, latency) of a communication path are usually aggregated from these underlying networks.

A communication path connects two or more nodes. A communication path is realized by one or more networks. A communication path is atomic.

Figure 35: Communication Path Notation, as Connection and as Box

Example

In the model below, we see a communication path "message queuing" between an Application Server and a Client.

Example 27: Communication Path

6.3 Behavioral Concepts

An *infrastructure service* describes the externally visible and accessible functionality of a node.

System software (similar to the "execution environment" concept of UML 2.0, but with a slightly broader interpretation) represents the software environment for specific types of components and data objects that are deployed on it in the form of artifacts.

6.3.1 Infrastructure Service

An infrastructure service is defined as an externally visible unit of functionality, provided by one or more nodes, exposed through well-defined interfaces, and meaningful to the environment.

An infrastructure service exposes the functionality of a node to its environment. This functionality is accessed through one or more infrastructure interfaces. It may require, use, and produce artifacts.

An infrastructure service should be meaningful from the point of view of the environment; it should provide a unit of functionality that is in itself useful to its users, such as application components and nodes.

Typical infrastructure services may, for example, include messaging, storage, naming, and directory services. It may access artifacts; e.g., a file containing a message.

An infrastructure service may be used by application components or nodes. An infrastructure service is realized by a node. An infrastructure service is exposed by a node by assigning it to its infrastructure interfaces. An infrastructure service may access artifacts.

The name of an infrastructure service should preferably be a verb ending with "-ing"; e.g., "messaging". Also, a name explicitly containing the word "service" may be used.

An infrastructure service may consist of sub-services.

Figure 36: Infrastructure Interface Notation

Example
In the model below, we see a Messaging service realized by Websphere MQ system software.

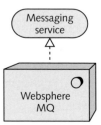

Example 28: Infrastructure Interface

6.3.2 System Software

> System software represents a software environment for specific types of
> components and objects that are deployed on it in the form of artifacts.

System software is a specialization of a node that is used to model the
software environment in which artifacts run. This can be, for example, an
operating system, a J2EE application server, a CORBA ORB, a database
system, a workflow engine, or COTS software such as ERP or CRM packages.
Also, system software can be used to represent, for example, communication
middleware. Usually, system software is combined with a device representing
the hardware environment to form a general node.

System software can be assigned to a device. Artifacts can be assigned to (i.e.,
deployed on) system software. A node can contain system software.

The name of system software should preferably be a noun referring to
the type of execution environment; e.g., "J2EE server". System software
may contain other system software; e.g., an operating system containing a
database.

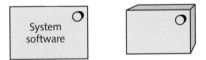

Figure 37: System Software Notation

> **Example**
> In the model below, we see DB2 system software assigned to (deployed on) an
> OS/390 mainframe device.

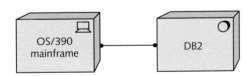

Example 29: System Software

6.4 Informational Concepts

An *artifact* is a physical piece of information that is used or produced in a software development process, or by deployment and operation of a system. It is the representation, in the form of, for example, a file, of a data object, or an application component, and can be deployed on a node. The artifact concept has been taken from UML 2.0.

6.4.1 Artifact

> An artifact is defined as a physical piece of information that is used or produced in a software development process, or by deployment and operation of a system.

An artifact represents a concrete element in the physical world. It is typically used to model (software) products such as source files, executables, scripts, database tables, messages, documents, specifications, and model files. An instance (copy) of an artifact can be deployed on a node.

An application component may be realized by one or more artifacts. A data object may be realized by one or more artifacts. An artifact may be assigned to (i.e., deployed on) a node. Thus, the two typical ways to use the artifact concept are as an *execution component* or as a *data file*. In fact, these could be defined as specializations of the artifact concept.

The name of an artifact should preferably be the name of the file it represents; e.g., "order.jar". An artifact may consist of sub-artifacts.

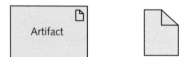

Figure 38: Artifact Notation

> **Example**
>
> In the example below, we see an artifact Risk management EJB, which represents a deployable unit of code, assigned to (deployed on) an application server.

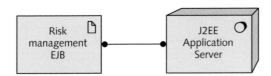

Example 30: Artifact

6.5 Summary of Technology Layer Concepts

Table 3 gives an overview of the concepts at the technology layer, with their definitions.

Table 3: Technology Layer Concepts

Concept	Definition	Notation
Node	A computational resource upon which artifacts may be deployed for execution.	Node
Device	A physical computational resource upon which artifacts may be deployed for execution.	Device
Network	A physical communication medium between two or more devices.	Network ⟷
Communication path	A link between two or more nodes, through which these nodes can exchange information.	Communication path
Infrastructure interface	A point of access where the functionality offered by a node can be accessed by other nodes and application components.	Infrastructure interface
System software	A software environment for specific types of components and objects that are deployed on it in the form of artifacts.	System software

Concept	Definition	Notation
Infrastructure service	An externally visible unit of functionality, provided by one or more nodes, exposed through well-defined interfaces, and meaningful to the environment.	Infrastructure service
Artifact	A physical piece of information that is used or produced in a software development process, or by deployment and operation of a system.	Artifact

Chapter 7

Cross-Layer Dependencies

In the previous chapters we have presented the concepts to model the business, application, and technology layers of an enterprise. However, a central issue in enterprise architecture is business-IT alignment: how can these layers be matched? In this chapter, we describe the relationships that the ArchiMate language offers to model the link between business, applications, and technology.

7.1 Business-Application Alignment

Figure 39 shows the relationships between business layer and application layer concepts. There are three main types of relationships between these layers:

1. *Used by* relationships, between application service and the different types of business behavior elements, and between application interface and business role. These relationships represent the behavioral and structural aspects of the support of the business by applications.
2. A *realization* relationship from a data object to a business object, to indicate that the data object is a digital representation of the corresponding business object.
3. *Assignment* relationships, between application component and the different types of business behavior elements, and between application interface and business service, to indicate that, for example, business processes or business services are completely automated.

In addition, there may be an aggregation relationship between a product and an application service, to indicate that the application service can be offered directly to a customer as part of the product.

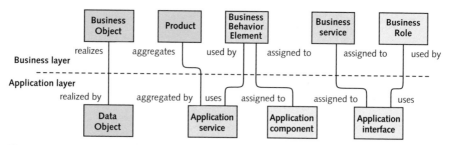

Figure 39: Relationships between Business Layer and Application Layer Concepts

Note: This figure does not show all permitted relationships: there are indirect
relationships that can be derived as explained in Section 8.5.

7.2 Application-Technology Alignment

Figure 40 shows the relationships between application layer and technology
layer concepts. There are two types of relationships between these layers:

1. *Used by* relationships, between infrastructure service and the different
   types of application behavior elements, and between infrastructure
   interface and application component. These relationships represent the
   behavioral and structural aspects of the use of technical infrastructure by
   applications.

2. A *realization* relationship from artifact to data object, to indicate that
   the data object is realized by, for example, a physical data file, and from
   artifact to application component, to indicate that a physical data file is
   an executable that realizes an application or part of an application. (Note:
   In this case, an artifact represents a "physical" component that is deployed
   on a node; this is modeled with an assignment relationship. A (logical)
   application component is realized by an artifact and, indirectly, by the
   node on which the artifact is deployed.)

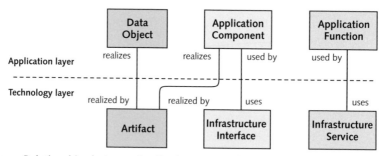

Figure 40: Relationships between Application Layer and Technology Layer Concepts

Note: This figure does not show all permitted relationships: there are indirect
relationships that can be derived as explained in Section 8.5.

Due to the derived relationships that are explained in Section 8.5, it is also
possible to draw relationships directly between the business and technology
layers. For example, if a business object is realized by a data object, which
in turn is realized by an artifact, this artifact indirectly realizes the business
object.

Chapter 8

Relationships

The metamodels and examples from the previous chapters show the different types of relationships that the ArchiMate language offers. In this chapter, we provide a more precise description of these relationships.

The relationships can be classified as either:
- *Structural*, which model the structural coherence of concepts of the same or different types
- *Dynamic*, which are used to model (temporal) dependencies between behavioral concepts
- *Other*, which do not fall in one of the two above categories

8.1 Structural Relationships

8.1.1 Composition Relationship

> The composition relationship indicates that an object consists of a number of other objects.

The composition relationship has been inspired by the composition relationship in UML class diagrams, but is applicable to compose a wider range of concepts. In contrast to the aggregation relationship, an object can be part of only one composition.

In addition to composition relationships that are explicitly defined in the metamodel figures of the previous sections, composition is always possible between two instances of the same concept.

Figure 41: Composition Notation

Alternatively, a composition relationship can be expressed by nesting the model elements.

> **Example**
>
> The models below show the two ways to express that the application component Financial application is composed of three other application components.

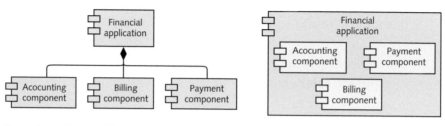

Example 31: Composition

8.1.2 Aggregation Relationship

> The aggregation relationship indicates that a concept groups a number of other concepts.

The aggregation relationship has been inspired on the aggregation relationship in UML class diagrams, but is applicable to aggregate a wider range of concepts. In contrast to the composition relationship, an object can be part of more than one aggregation.

In addition to aggregation relationships that are explicitly defined in the metamodel figures of the previous sections, aggregation is always possible between two instances of the same concept.

Figure 42: Aggregation Notation

Alternatively, an aggregation relationship can be expressed by nesting the model elements.

> **Example**
>
> The models below show the two ways to express that the product Car insurance aggregates a contract (Policy) and two business services.

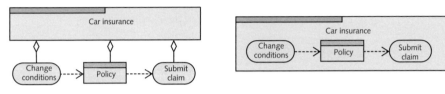

Example 32: Aggregation

8.1.3 Assignment Relationship

> The assignment relationship links active elements (e.g., business roles or application components) with units of behavior that are performed by them, or business actors with business roles that are fulfilled by them.

The assignment relationship can relate a business role with a business process or function, an application component with an application function, a business collaboration with a business interaction, an application collaboration with an application interaction, a business interface with a business service, an application interface with an application service, or a business actor with a business role.

Figure 43: Assignment Notation

Alternatively, an assignment relationship can be expressed by nesting the model elements.

> **Example**
>
> The model in below includes the two ways to express the assignment relationship. The Payment function (application) is assigned to the Financial application (component), and the Payment service (application) is assigned to the Application interface.

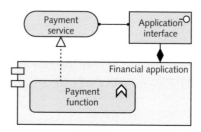

Example 33: Assignment

8.1.4 Realization Relationship

The realization relationship links a logical entity with a more concrete entity that realizes it.

The realization relationship indicates how logical entities ("what"), such as services, are realized by means of more concrete entities ("how"). The realization relationship is used in an operational sense (e.g., a process/function realizes a service), but also in a design/implementation context (e.g., a data object may realize a business object, or an artifact may realize an application component).

Figure 44: Realization Notation

Example

The model below illustrates two ways to use the realization relationship. An application (component) Financial application realizes the Billing service (application); the Billing data object realizes the business object Invoice.

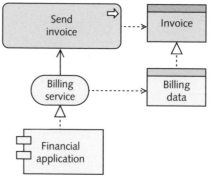

Example 34: Realization

8.1.5 Used By Relationship

> The used by relationship models the use of services by processes, functions, or
> interactions and the access to interfaces by roles, components, or collaborations.

The used by relationship describes the services that a role or component
offers that are used by entities in the environment. The used by relationship is
applied for both the behavior aspect and the structure aspect.

Figure 45: Used By Notation

> **Example**
> The model below illustrates the used by relationship: an application interface
> (in this case, the user interface of the application) is used by the Front office
> employee, while the Update customer info service is used in the Process change of
> address business process.

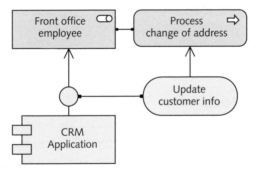

Example 35: Used By

8.1.6 Access Relationship

> The access relationship models the access of behavioral concepts to business or
> data objects.

The access relationship indicates that a process, function, interaction, service, or event "does something" with a (business or data) object; e.g., create a new object, read data from the object, write or modify the object data, or delete the object. The relationship can also be used to indicate that the object is just associated with the behavior; e.g., it models the information that comes with an event, or the information that is made available as part of a service. The arrow indicates the flow of information.

Figure 46: Access Notation

> **Example**
> The model below illustrates the access relationship: the Create invoice sub-process writes/creates the Invoice business object; the Send invoice sub-process reads the Invoice business object.

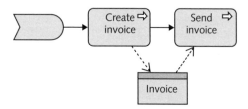

Example 36: Access

8.1.7 Association Relationship

> An association models a relationship between objects that is not covered by another, more specific relationship.

Association is mainly used, as in UML, to model relationships between business objects or data objects that are not modeled by the standard relationships aggregation, composition, or specialization. In addition to this, the association relationship is used to link the informational concepts with the other concepts: a business object with a representation, a representation with a meaning, and a business service with a purpose.

——————

Figure 47: Association Notation

Example

The model illustrates a number of uses of the association relationship.

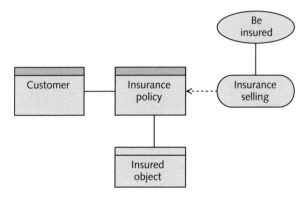

Example 37: Association

8.2 Dynamic Relationships

8.2.1 Triggering Relationship

The triggering relationship describes the temporal or causal relations between processes, functions, interactions, and events.

The triggering relationship is used to model the causal relationships between behavior concepts in a process. No distinction is made between an active triggering relationship and a passive causal relationship.

——————▶

Figure 48: Triggering Notation

Example

The model below illustrates that triggering relationships are mostly used to model causal dependencies between (sub-)processes and/or events.

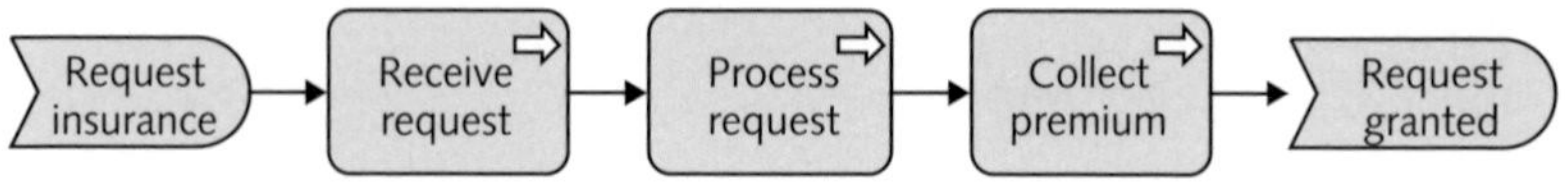

Example 38: Triggering

8.2.2 Flow Relationship

The flow relationship describes the exchange or transfer of, for example, information or value between processes, function, interactions, and events.

The flow relationship is used to model the flow of, for example, information between behavior concepts in a process. A flow relationship does not imply a causal or temporal relationship.

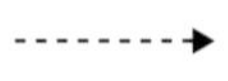

Figure 49: Flow Notation

Example
The model below shows a Claim assessment business function, which forwards decisions about the claims to the Claim settlement business function. In order to determine the order in which the claims should be assessed, Claim assessment makes use of schedule information received from the Scheduling business function.

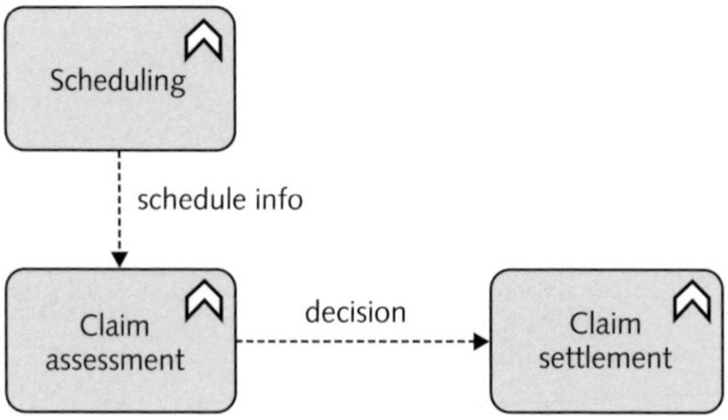

Example 39: Flow

8.3 Other Relationships

8.3.1 Grouping

> The grouping relationship indicates that objects belong together based on some common characteristic.

Similar to the UML package, the grouping relationship is used to group an arbitrary group of model objects, which can be of the same type or of different types. In contrast to the aggregation or composition relationships, there is no "overall" object of which the grouped objects form a part.

Figure 50: Grouping Notation

Unlike the other language concepts, grouping has no formal semantics. It is only used to show graphically that model elements have something in common. Model elements may belong to multiple (overlapping) groups.

Example
In the model below, the grouping relationship is used to group business objects that belong to the same information domain, in this case Financial administration.

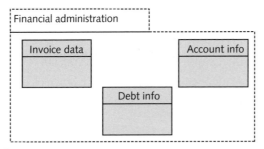

Example 40: Grouping

8.3.2 Junction

> A junction is used to connect dynamic relationships of the same type.

A junction is used in a number of situations to connect dynamic (triggering or flow) relationships of the same type; e.g., to indicate splits or joins.

●

Figure 51: Junction Notation

> **Example**
> In the model below, a junction is used to denote an *or*-split (choice).

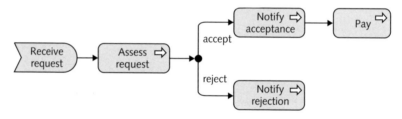

Example 41: Junction

8.3.3 Specialization Relationship

> The specialization relationship indicates that an object is a specialization of another object.

The specialization relationship has been inspired by the generalization/specialization relationship in UML class diagrams, but is applicable to specialize a wider range of concepts. The specialization relationship can relate any instance of a concept with another instance of the same concept.

Specialization is always possible between two instances of the same concept.

Figure 52: Specialization Notation

Example

The model below illustrates the use of the specialization relationship for a
business process. In this case the Take out travel insurance and Take out luggage
insurance processes are a specialization of a more generic insurance take out
process.

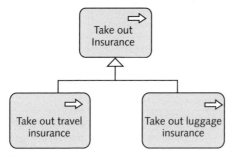

Example 42: Specialization

8.4 Summary of Relationships

Table 4 gives an overview of the ArchiMate relationships with their
definitions.

Table 4: Relationships

Structural Relationships		Notation
Association	Association models a relationship between objects that is not covered by another, more specific relationship.	———
Access	The access relationship models the access of behavioral concepts to business or data objects.	╌╌╌╌╌> ╌╌╌╌╌
Used by	The used by relationship models the use of services by processes, functions, or interactions and the access to interfaces by roles, components, or collaborations.	———>

Structural Relationships		Notation
Realization	The realization relationship links a logical entity with a more concrete entity that realizes it.	------ ▷
Assignment	The assignment relationship links units of behavior with active elements (e.g., roles, components) that perform them, or roles with actors that fulfill them.	●——————●
Aggregation	The aggregation relationship indicates that an object groups a number of other objects.	◇——————
Composition	The composition relationship indicates that an object consists of a number of other objects.	◆——————
Dynamic Relationships		**Notation**
Flow	The flow relationship describes the exchange or transfer of, for example, information or value between processes, function, interactions, and events.	- - - - - ▶
Triggering	The triggering relationship describes the temporal or causal relations between processes, functions, interactions, and events.	————▶
Other Relationships		**Notation**
Grouping	The grouping relationship indicates that objects, of the same type or different types, belong together based on some common characteristic.	▯
Junction	A junction is used to connect relationships of the same type.	●
Specialization	The specialization relationship indicates that an object is a specialization of another object.	◁——————

8.5 Derived Relationships

The structural relationships described in the previous sections form an important category of relations to describe coherence. The structural relationships are listed in Table 4 in ascending order by "strength": association is the weakest structural relationship; composition is the strongest. Part of the language definition is an abstraction rule that states that two relationships that join at an intermediate element can be combined and replaced by the weaker of the two.

> If two structural relationships $r{:}R$ and $s{:}S$ are permitted between elements a, b, and c such that $r(a,b)$ and $s(b,c)$, then a structural relationship $t{:}T$ is also permitted, with $t(a,c)$ and type T being the weakest of R and S.

Transitively applying this property allows us to replace a "chain" of structural relationships (with intermediate model elements) by the weakest structural relationship in the chain. For a more formal description and derivation of this rule we refer to [15].

With this rule, it is possible to determine the "indirect" relationships that exist between model elements without a direct relationship, which may be useful for, among other things, impact analysis. An example is shown in Figure 43: assume that we would like to know what the impact on the client is if the CRM system fails. In this case, an indirect "used by" relation (the thick arrow on the left) can be derived from this system to the Claim registration service (from the chain assignment – used by – realization – used by – realization). No indirect (structural) relationship is drawn between the CRM system and the Claims payment service.

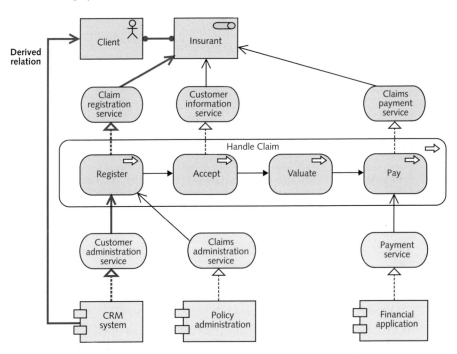

Example 43: Derived Relationship

It is important to note that all these derived relationships are also valid in ArchiMate. These are not shown in the "barebones" metamodel illustrations shown in the previous sections, because this would clutter up the diagrams. However, the table in Appendix B shows all permitted relationships between two elements in the language.

Architecture Viewpoints

9.1 Introduction

Establishing and maintaining a coherent enterprise architecture is clearly a complex task, because it involves many different people with differing backgrounds using various notations. In order to get a handle on this complexity, researchers have initially focused on the definition of architectural frameworks for classifying and positioning the various architectural descriptions with respect to each other (e.g., the Zachman framework [5], [9]). A problem with looking at enterprise architecture through the lens of an architectural framework is that it categorizes and divides architectural descriptions rather than providing insight into their coherence.

ArchiMate advocates a more flexible approach in which architects and other stakeholders can define their own views on the enterprise architecture. In this approach, views are specified by *viewpoints*. Viewpoints define abstractions on the set of models representing the enterprise architecture, each aimed at a particular type of stakeholder and addressing a particular set of concerns. Viewpoints can both be used to view certain aspects in isolation, and for relating two or more aspects.

The notion of viewpoint-oriented architecture has been around for a while in requirements and software engineering. In the 1990s, a substantial number of researchers worked on what was phrased as "the multiple perspectives problem" [16], [17]. By this term they referred to the problem of how to organize and guide (software) development in a setting with many actors, using diverse representation schemes, having diverse domain knowledge and different development strategies. A general framework has been developed in order to address the diverse issues related to this problem [16], [17]. In this framework, a viewpoint combines the notion of "actor", "role", or "agent" in the development process with the idea of a "perspective" or "view" which an actor maintains. More precisely, viewpoints are defined as loosely coupled, locally managed, distributable objects; thus containing identity, state, and behavior. A viewpoint is more than a "partial specification"; in addition, it contains partial knowledge of how to develop that partial specification. These early ideas on viewpoint-oriented software engineering have found their way into ISO/IEC 42010:2007 [2] on which we have based our definitions below.

As a result of these ideas, several architecture frameworks can be found in the field of literature, which are essentially viewpoint classification schemes. For example, the Zachman framework [5], [9] divides the enterprise architecture into 36 different enterprise-wide "architectures" (i.e., viewpoints). Tapscott and Caston's framework [18] distinguishes five different and complementing viewpoints: business, work, information, application, and technology. Kruchten [19] introduces the "4+1" method, in which four views (logic, process, development, and physical), each having its own notation, are coupled through a fifth view: the scenario view illustrating the collaboration between the other four views.

Viewpoints are also prominently present in the ISO standardized Reference Model for Open Distributed Processing (RM-ODP) [7]. The RM-ODP identifies five viewpoints from which to specify ODP systems, each focusing on a particular area of concern; i.e., enterprise, information, computational, engineering, and technology. It is claimed that the ODP viewpoints form a necessary and sufficient set to meet the needs of ODP standards. More recently, the term "viewpoint" is also used in OMG's Model Driven Architecture (MDA) initiative to refer to the different model types; i.e., Platform-Independent Model (PIM) and Platform-Specific Model (PSM) [20]. Hence, we conclude that the use of viewpoints and architectural views are well-established concepts in software architecture.

In the domain of enterprise architecture, the TOGAF framework describes a taxonomy of views for different categories of stakeholders. Next to this description of views, TOGAF also provides guidelines for the development and use of viewpoints and views in enterprise architecture models.

The views and viewpoints proposed by any of the above mentioned frameworks should not be considered in isolation: views are inter-related and, often, it is exactly a combination of views together with their underlying inter-dependency relationships the best way to describe and communicate a piece of architecture. It should, however, be noted that views and viewpoints have a limiting character. They are eventually a restriction of the whole system (and architecture) to a partial number of aspects – a view is just a partial incomplete depiction of the system.

9.2 Views, Viewpoints, and Stakeholders

Views are an ideal mechanism to purposefully convey information about architecture areas. In general, a *view* is defined as a part of an architecture description that addresses a set of related concerns and is addressed to a set of stakeholders. A view is specified by means of a *viewpoint*, which prescribes the concepts, models, analysis techniques, and visualizations that are provided by the view. Simply put, a view is what you see, and a viewpoint is where you are looking from.

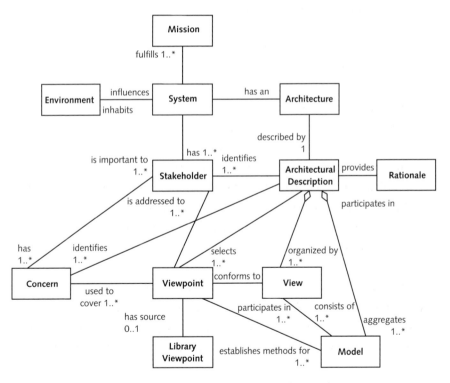

Figure 53: Conceptual Model of Architectural Description (from [2])

Viewpoints are a means to focus on particular aspects of the architecture. These aspects are determined by the concerns of a stakeholder with whom communication takes place. What should and should not be visible from a specific viewpoint is therefore entirely dependent on the argumentation with respect to a stakeholder's concerns.

Viewpoints are designed for the purpose of communicating certain aspects of an architecture. The communication enabled by a viewpoint can be strictly informative, but in general will be bi-directional. The architect informs stakeholders, and stakeholders give their feedback (critique or consent) on the presented aspects. What is and what is not shown in a view depends on the scope of the viewpoint and on what is relevant to the concerns of the stakeholder. Ideally, these are the same; i.e., the viewpoint is designed with specific concerns of a stakeholder in mind. Relevance to a stakeholder's concern, therefore, is *the* selection criterion that is used to determine which objects and relations are to appear in a view.

The following are examples of stakeholders and concerns as a basis for the specification of viewpoints:

- *End user*: For example, what are the consequences for his work and workplace?
- *Architect*: What is the consequence for the maintainability of a system, with respect to corrective, preventive, and adaptive maintenance?
- *Upper-level management*: How can we ensure our policies are followed in the development and operation of processes and systems? What is the impact of decisions (on personnel, finance, ICT, etc.)?
- *Operational manager*, responsible for exploitation or maintenance: For example, what new technologies are there to prepare for? Is there a need to adapt maintenance processes? What is the impact of changes to existing applications? How secure are my systems?
- *Project manager*, responsible for the development of new applications: What are the relevant domains and their relations? What is the dependence of business processes on the applications to be built? What is their expected performance?
- *Developer*: What are the modifications with respect to the current situation that need to be done?

9.3 Viewpoint Classification

An architect is confronted with many different types of stakeholders and concerns. To help him in selecting the right viewpoints for the task at hand, we introduce a framework for the definition and classification of viewpoints and views. The framework is based on two dimensions: *purpose* and *content*. The following three types of architecture support the purpose dimension of architecture views:

- *Designing*: Design viewpoints support architects and designers in the design process from initial sketch to detailed design. Typically, design viewpoints consist of diagrams, like those used in, for example, UML.
- *Deciding*: Decision support viewpoints assist managers in the process of decision-making by offering insight into cross-domain architecture relations, typically through projections and intersections of underlying models, but also by means of analytical techniques. Typical examples are cross-reference tables, landscape maps, lists, and reports.
- *Informing*: Informing viewpoints help to inform any stakeholder about the enterprise architecture, in order to achieve understanding, obtain commitment, and convince adversaries. Typical examples are illustrations, animations, cartoons, flyers, etc.

The goal of this classification is to assist architects and others find suitable viewpoints given their task at hand; i.e., the purpose that a view must serve and the content it should display. With the help of this framework, it is easier to find typical viewpoints that might be useful in a given situation. This implies that we do not provide an orthogonal categorization of each viewpoint into one of three classes; these categories are not exclusive in the sense that a viewpoint in one category cannot be applied to achieve another type of support. For instance, some decision support viewpoints may be used to communicate to any other stakeholders as well.

For characterizing the content of a view we define the following abstraction levels:

- *Details*: Views on the detailed level typically consider one layer and one aspect from the ArchiMate framework. Typical stakeholders are a software engineer responsible for design and implementation of a software component or a process owner responsible for effective and efficient process execution. Examples of views are a BPMN process diagram and a UML class diagram.
- *Coherence*: At the coherence abstraction level, multiple layers or multiple aspects are spanned. Extending the view to more than one layer or aspect enables the stakeholder to focus on architecture relations like process-

uses-system (multiple layer) or application-uses-object (multiple aspect). Typical stakeholders are operational managers responsible for a collection of IT services or business processes.

• *Overview*: The overview abstraction level addresses both multiple layers and multiple aspects. Typically, such overviews are addressed to enterprise architects and decision-makers, such as CEOs and CIOs.

In Figure 54, the dimensions of purpose and abstraction level are visualized in a single picture, together with examples of stakeholders. Table 5 and Table 6 summarize the different purposes and abstraction levels.

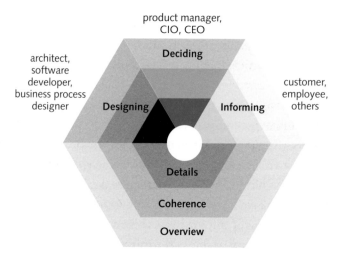

Figure 54: Classification of Enterprise Architecture Viewpoints

Table 5: Viewpoint Purpose

	Typical Stakeholders	Purpose	Examples
Designing	architect, software developer, business process designer	navigate, design, support design decisions, compare alternatives	UML diagram, BPMN diagram, flowchart, ER diagram
Deciding	manager, CIO, CEO	decision-making	cross-reference table, landscape map, list, report
Informing	employee, customer, others	explain, convince, obtain commitment	animation, cartoon, process illustration, chart

Table 6: Viewpoint Abstraction Levels

	Typical Stakeholders	**Purpose**	**Examples**
Details	software engineer, process owner	design, manage	UML class diagram, BPMN process diagram
Coherence	operational managers	analyze dependencies, impact of-change	views expressing relations like "use", "realize", and "assign"
Overview	enterprise architect, CIO, CEO	change management	landscape map

9.4 Basic Viewpoints in ArchiMate

The basic viewpoint in ArchiMate is a selection of a relevant subset of the ArchiMate concepts (and their relations) and the representation of that part of an architecture that is expressed in different diagrams. A set of such viewpoints was developed based on practical experience. Some of these viewpoints have a scope that is limited to a single layer or aspect. Thus, the Business Function and Business Process viewpoints show the two main perspectives on the business behavior; the Organization viewpoint depicts the structure of the enterprise in terms of its departments, roles, etc.; the Information Structure viewpoint describes the information and data used; the Application Structure, Behavior, and Co-operation viewpoints contain the applications and components and their mutual relations; and the Infrastructure viewpoint shows the infrastructure and platforms underlying the enterprise's information systems in terms of networks, devices, and system software. Other viewpoints link multiple layers and/or aspects: the Actor Co-operation and Product viewpoints relate the enterprise to its environment; the Application Usage viewpoint relates applications to their use in, for example, business processes; and the Deployment viewpoint shows how applications are mapped onto the underlying infrastructure.

In the following sections, all ArchiMate viewpoints are separately described in detail. For each viewpoint the comprised concepts and relations, the guidelines for the viewpoint use, and the goal and target group and of the viewpoint are indicated. Furthermore, each viewpoint description contains example models. For more details on the goal and use of viewpoints, refer to [3], Chapter 7.

9.4.1 Introductory Viewpoint

The Introductory viewpoint forms a subset of the full ArchiMate language using a simplified notation. It is typically used at the start of a design trajectory, when not everything needs to be detailed yet, or to explain the essence of an architecture model to non-architects that require a simpler notation. Another use of this basic, less formal viewpoint is that it tries to avoid the impression that the architectural design is already fixed, an idea that may easily arise when using a more formal, highly structured or detailed visualization.

We use a simplified notation for the concepts, and for the relations. All relations except "triggering" and "realization" are denoted by simple lines; "realization" has an arrow in the direction of the realized service; "triggering" is also represented by an arrow. The concepts are denoted with slightly thicker lines and rounded corners, which give a less formal impression. The example below illustrates this notation. On purpose, the layout of this example is not as "straight" as an ordinary architecture diagram; this serves to avoid the idea that the design is already fixed.

Table 7: Introductory Viewpoint Description

Introductory Viewpoint		
Stakeholders	Enterprise architects, managers	
Concerns	Make design choices visible, convince stakeholders	
Purpose	Designing, deciding, informing	
Abstraction Level	Coherence, Overview, Detail	
Layer	Business, Application, and Technology layers (see also Figure 5)	
Aspects	Structure, behavior, information (see also Figure 5)	

Concepts and Relations

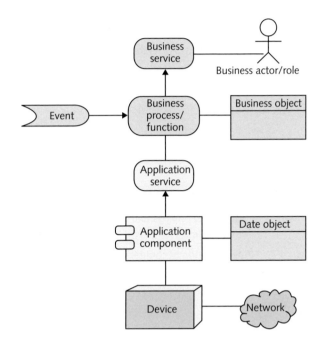

Example

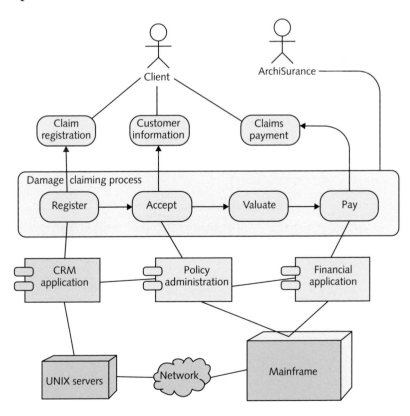

9.4.2 Organization Viewpoint

The Organization viewpoint focuses on the (internal) organization of a company, a department, a network of companies, or of another organizational entity. It is possible to present models in this viewpoint as nested block diagrams, but also in a more traditional way, such as organizational charts. The Organization viewpoint is very useful in identifying competencies, authority, and responsibilities in an organization.

Table 8: Organization Viewpoint Description

Organization Viewpoint	
Stakeholders	Enterprise, process and domain architects, managers, employees, shareholders
Concerns	Identification of competencies, authority, and responsibilities
Purpose	Designing, deciding, informing
Abstraction Level	Coherence
Layer	Business layer (see also Figure 5)
Aspects	Structure (see also Figure 5)

Concepts and Relations

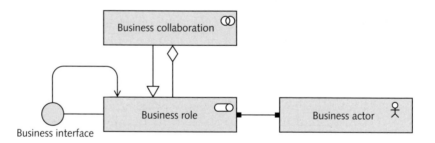

Example

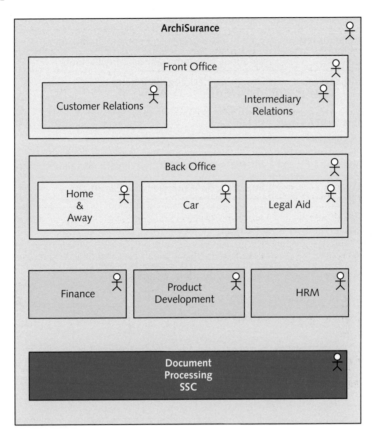

9.4.3 Actor Co-operation Viewpoint

The Actor Co-operation viewpoint focuses on the relations of actors with each other and their environment. A common example of this is the "context diagram", which puts an organization into its environment, consisting of external parties such as customers, suppliers, and other business partners. It is very useful in determining external dependencies and collaborations and shows the value chain or network in which the actor operates.

Another important use of the Actor Co-operation viewpoint is in showing how a number of co-operating business actors and/or application components together realize a business process. Hence, in this view, both business actors or roles and application components may occur.

Table 9: Actor Co-operation Viewpoint Description

Actor Co-operation Viewpoint	
Stakeholders	Enterprise, process, and domain architects
Concerns	Relations of actors with their environment
Purpose	Designing, deciding, informing
Abstraction Level	Detail
Layer	Business layer (application layer) (see also Figure 5)
Aspects	Structure, behavior (see also Figure 5)

Concepts and Relations

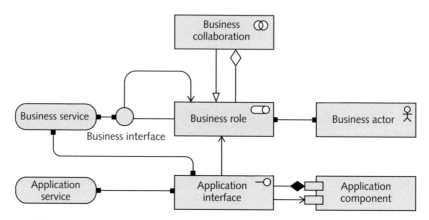

Example

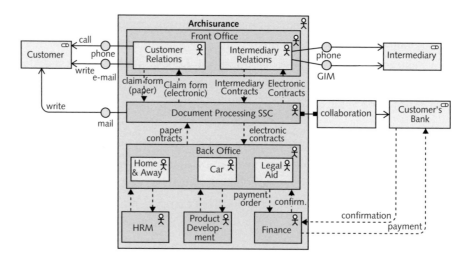

9.4.4 Business Function Viewpoint

The Business Function viewpoint shows the main business functions of an organization and their relations in terms of the flows of information, value, or goods between them. Business functions are used to represent the most stable aspects of a company in terms of the primary activities it performs, regardless of organizational changes or technological developments. Therefore, the business function architecture of companies that operate in the same market often exhibit close similarities. The business function viewpoint thus provides high-level insight in the general operations of the company, and can be used to identify necessary competencies, or to structure an organization according to its main activities.

Table 10: Business Function Viewpoint Description

Business Function Viewpoint	
Stakeholders	Enterprise, process, and domain architects
Concerns	Identification of competencies, identification of main activities, reduction of complexity
Purpose	Designing
Abstraction Level	Coherence
Layer	Business layer (see also Figure 5)
Aspects	Behavior, structure (see also Figure 5)

Concepts and Relations

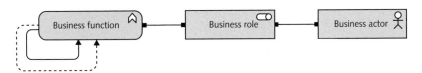

Example

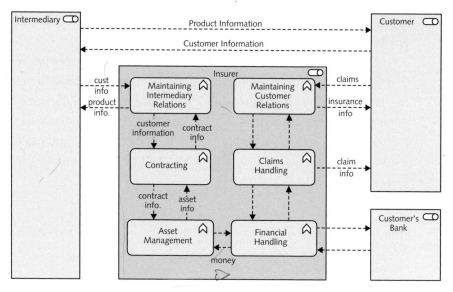

9.4.5 Business Process Viewpoint

The Business Process viewpoint is used to show the high-level structure and composition of one or more business processes. Next to the processes themselves, this viewpoint contains other directly related concepts, such as:

- The services a business process offers to the outside world, showing how a process contributes to the realization of the company's products
- The assignment of business processes to roles, which gives insight into the responsibilities of the associated actors
- The information used by the business process

Each of these can be regarded as a "sub-view" of the business process view.

Table 11: Business Process Viewpoint Description

Business Process Viewpoint			
Stakeholders	Process and domain architects, operational managers		
Concerns	Structure of business processes, consistency and completeness, responsibilities		
Purpose	Designing		
Abstraction Level	Detail		
Layer	Business layer (see also Figure 5)		
Aspects	Behavior (see also Figure 5)		

Concepts and Relations

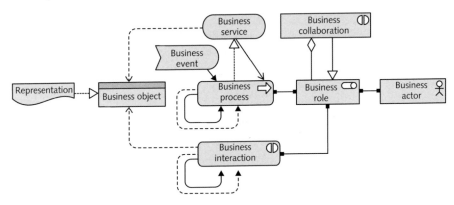

Example

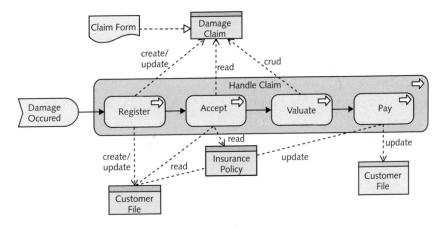

9.4.6 Business Process Co-operation Viewpoint

The Business Process Co-operation viewpoint is used to show the relations of one or more business processes with each other and/or with their environment. It can both be used to create a high-level design of business processes within their context and to provide an operational manager responsible for one or more such processes with insight into their dependencies. Important aspects of business process co-operation are:

- Causal relations between the main business processes of the enterprise
- Mapping of business processes onto business functions
- Realization of services by business processes
- Use of shared data
- Execution of a business process by the same roles or actors

Each of these can be regarded as a "sub-view" of the business process co-operation view.

Table 12: Business Process Co-operation Viewpoint Description

Business Process Co-operation Viewpoint	
Stakeholders	Process and domain architects, operational managers
Concerns	Dependencies between business processes, consistency and completeness, responsibilities
Purpose	Designing, deciding
Abstraction Level	Coherence
Layer	Business layer, application layer (see also Figure 5)
Aspects	Behavior (see also Figure 5)

Concepts and Relations

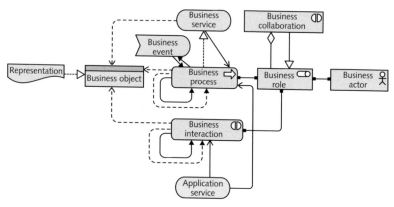

Example

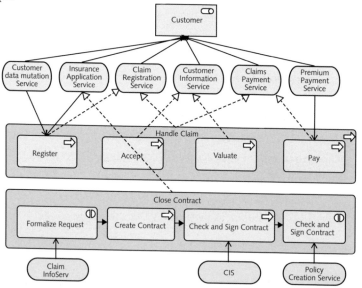

9.4.7 Product Viewpoint

The Product viewpoint depicts the value these products offer to the customers or other external parties involved and shows the composition of one or more products in terms of the constituting (business or application) services, and the associated contract(s) or other agreements. It may also be used to show the interfaces (channels) through which this product is offered, and the events associated with the product. A Product viewpoint is typically used in product development to design a product by composing existing services or by identifying which new services have to be created for this product, given the value a customer expects from it. It may then serve as input for business process architects and others that need to design the processes and ICT realizing these products.

Table 13: Product Viewpoint Description

Product Viewpoint	
Stakeholders	Product developers, product managers, process and domain architects
Concerns	Product development, value offered by the products of the enterprise
Purpose	Designing, deciding
Abstraction Level	Coherence
Layer	Business layer, application layer (see also Figure 5)
Aspects	Behavior, information (see also Figure 5)

Concepts and Relations

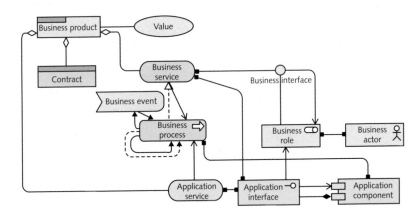

Example

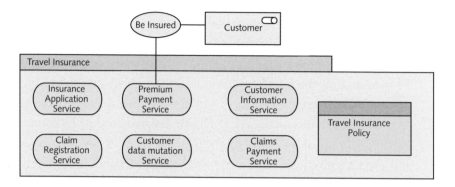

9.4.8 Application Behavior Viewpoint

The Application Behavior viewpoint describes the internal behavior of
an application; e.g., as it realizes one or more application services. This
viewpoint is useful in designing the main behavior of applications, or in
identifying functional overlap between different applications.

Table 14: Application Behavior Viewpoint Description

Application Behavior Viewpoint	
Stakeholders	Enterprise, process, application, and domain architects
Concerns	Structure, relations and dependencies between applications, consistency and completeness, reduction of complexity
Purpose	Designing
Abstraction Level	Coherence, details
Layer	Application layer (see also Figure 5)
Aspects	Information, behavior, structure (see also Figure 5)

Concepts and Relations

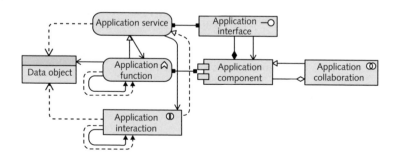

Example

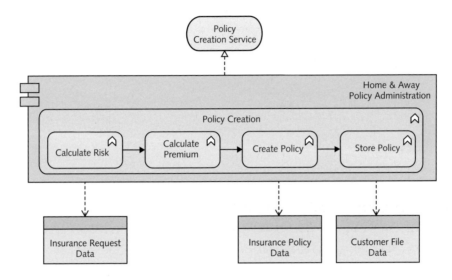

9.4.9 Application Co-operation Viewpoint

The Application Co-operation viewpoint describes the relations between applications components in terms of the information flows between them, or in terms of the services they offer and use. This viewpoint is typically used to create an overview of the application landscape of an organization. This viewpoint is also used to express the (internal) co-operation or orchestration of services that together support the execution of a business process.

Table 15: Application Co-operation Viewpoint Description

Application Co-operation Viewpoint	
Stakeholders	Enterprise , process, application, and domain architects
Concerns	Relations and dependencies between applications, orchestration/ choreography of services, consistency and completeness, reduction of complexity
Purpose	Designing
Abstraction Level	Coherence, details
Layer	Application layer (see also Figure 5)
Aspects	Behavior, structure (see also Figure 5)

Concepts and Relations

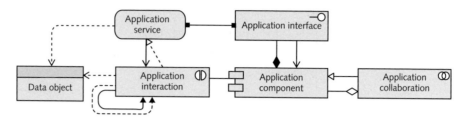

Example

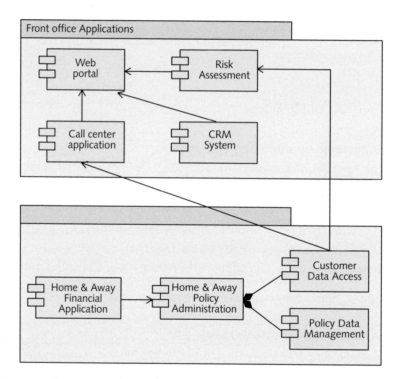

9.4.10 Application Structure Viewpoint

The Application Structure viewpoint shows the structure of one or more
applications or components. This viewpoint is useful in designing or
understanding the main structure of applications or components and
the associated data; e.g., to break down the structure of the system under
construction, or to identify legacy application components that are suitable
for migration/integration.

Table 16: Application Structure Viewpoint Description

Application Structure Viewpoint		
Stakeholders	Enterprise, process, application, and domain architects	
Concerns	Application structure, consistency and completeness, reduction of complexity	
Purpose	Designing	
Abstraction Level	Details	
Layer	Application layer (see also Figure 5)	
Aspects	Structure, information (see also Figure 5)	

Concepts and Relations

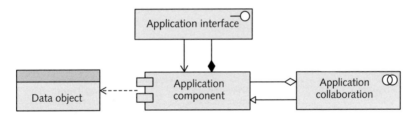

Example

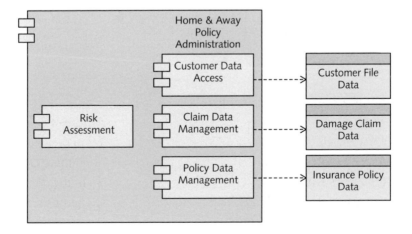

9.4.11 Application Usage Viewpoint

The Application Usage viewpoint describes how applications are used to support one or more business processes, and how they are used by other applications. It can be used in designing an application by identifying the services needed by business processes and other applications, or in designing business processes by describing the services that are available. Furthermore, since it identifies the dependencies of business processes upon applications, it may be useful to operational managers responsible for these processes.

Table 17: Application Usage Viewpoint Description

Application Usage Viewpoint	
Stakeholders	Enterprise, process, and application architects, operational managers
Concerns	Consistency and completeness, reduction of complexity
Purpose	Designing, deciding
Abstraction Level	Coherence
Layer	Business and application layers (see also Figure 5)
Aspects	Behavior, structure (see also Figure 5)

Concepts and Relations

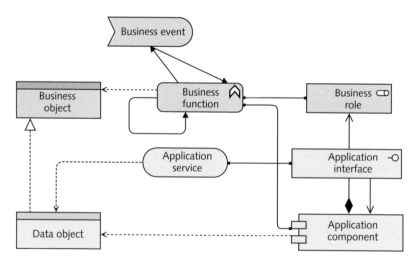

Example

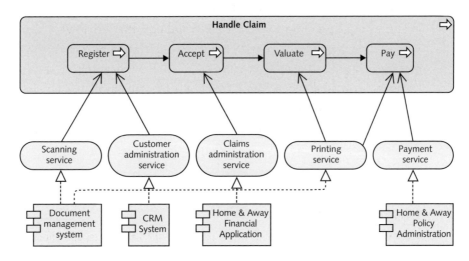

9.4.12 Infrastructure Viewpoint

The Infrastructure viewpoint contains the software and hardware infrastructure elements supporting the application layer, such as physical devices, networks, or system software (e.g., operating systems, databases, and middleware).

Table 18: Infrastructure Viewpoint Description

Infrastructure Viewpoint	
Stakeholders	Infrastructure architects, operational managers
Concerns	Stability, security, dependencies, costs of the infrastructure
Purpose	Designing
Abstraction Level	Details
Layer	Technology layer (see also Figure 5)
Aspects	Behavior, structure (see also Figure 5)

Concepts and Relations

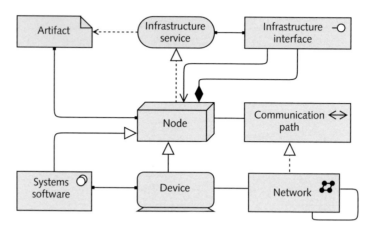

Example

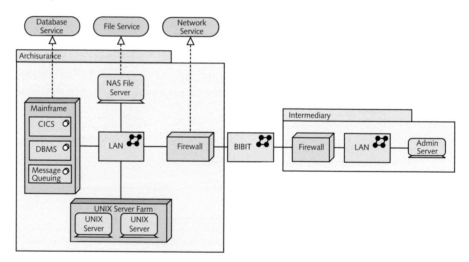

9.4.13 Infrastructure Usage Viewpoint

The Infrastructure Usage viewpoint shows how applications are supported by the software and hardware infrastructure: the infrastructure services are delivered by the devices; system software and networks are provided to the applications. This viewpoint plays an important role in the analysis of performance and scalability, since it relates the physical infrastructure to the logical world of applications. It is very useful in determining the performance and quality requirements on the infrastructure based on the demands of the various applications that use it.

Table 19: Infrastructure Usage Viewpoint Description

Infrastructure Usage Viewpoint		
Stakeholders	Application, infrastructure architects, operational managers	
Concerns	Dependencies, performance, scalability	
Purpose	Designing	
Abstraction Level	Coherence	
Layer	Application and technology layers (see also Figure 5)	
Aspects	Behavior, structure (see also Figure 5)	

Concepts and Relations

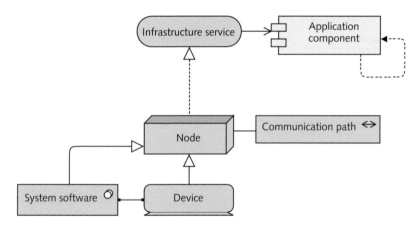

Example

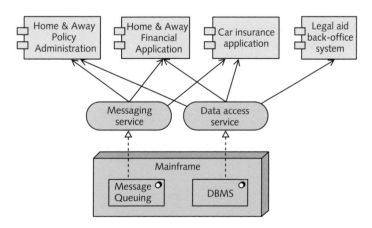

9.4.14 Implementation and Deployment Viewpoint

The Implementation and Deployment viewpoint shows how one or more applications are realized on the infrastructure. This comprises the mapping of (logical) applications and components onto (physical) artifacts, such as Enterprise Java Beans, and the mapping of the information used by these applications and components onto the underlying storage infrastructure; e.g., database tables or other files. Deployment views play an important role in the analysis of performance and scalability, since they relate the physical infrastructure to the logical world of applications. In security and risk analysis, deployment views are used to identify, for example, critical dependencies and risks.

Table 20: Implementation and Deployment Viewpoint Description

Implementation and Deployment Viewpoint		
Stakeholders	Application and infrastructure architects, operational managers	
Concerns	Dependencies, security, risks	
Purpose	Designing	
Abstraction Level	Coherence	
Layer	Application layer, technology layer (see also Figure 5)	
Aspects	Information, behavior, structure (see also Figure 5)	

Concepts and Relations

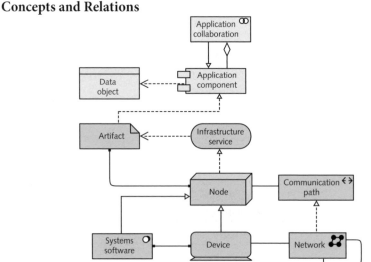

Example

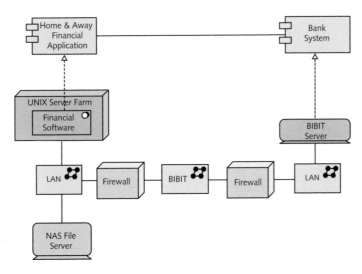

9.4.15 Information Structure Viewpoint

The Information Structure viewpoint is comparable to the traditional
information models created in the development of almost any information
system. It shows the structure of the information used in the enterprise or in
a specific business process or application, in terms of data types or (object-
oriented) class structures. Furthermore, it may show how the information
at the business level is represented at the application level in the form of
the data structures used there, and how these are then mapped onto the
underlying infrastructure; e.g., by means of a database schema.

Table 21: Information Structure Viewpoint Description

Information Structure Viewpoint	
Stakeholders	Domain and information architects
Concerns	Structure and dependencies of the used data and information, consistency and completeness
Purpose	Designing
Abstraction Level	Details
Layer	Business layer, application layer, technology layer (see also Figure 5)
Aspects	Information (see also Figure 5)

Concepts and Relations

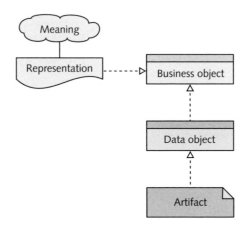

Example

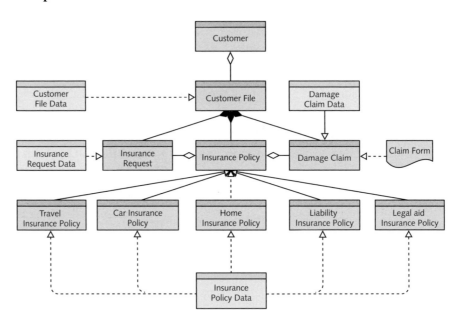

9.4.16 Service Realization Viewpoint

The Service Realization viewpoint is used to show how one or more business services are realized by the underlying processes (and sometimes by application components). Thus, it forms the bridge between the business products viewpoint and the business process view. It provides a "view from the outside" on one or more business processes.

Table 22: Service Realization Viewpoint Description

Service Realization Viewpoint		
Stakeholders	Process and domain architects, product and operational managers	
Concerns	Added-value of business processes, consistency and completeness, responsibilities	
Purpose	Designing, deciding	
Abstraction Level	Coherence	
Layer	Business layer (application layer) (see also Figure 5)	
Aspects	Behavior, structure, information (see also Figure 5)	

Concepts and Relations

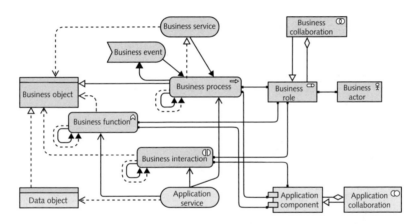

Example

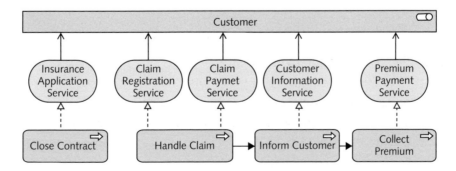

9.4.17 Layered Viewpoint

The Layered viewpoint pictures several layers and aspects of an enterprise architecture in one diagram. There are two categories of layers, namely *dedicated layers* and *service layers*. The layers are the result of the use of the "grouping" relation for a natural partitioning of the entire set of objects and relations that belong to a model. The infrastructure, the application, the process, and the actors/roles layers belong to the first category. The structural principle behind a fully layered viewpoint is that each dedicated layer exposes, by means of the "realization" relation a layer of services, which are further on "used by" the next dedicated layer. Thus, we can easily separate the internal structure and organization of a dedicated layer from its externally observable behavior expressed as the service layer that the dedicated layer realizes. The order, number, or nature of these layers are not fixed, but in general a (more or less) complete and natural layering of an ArchiMate model will contain the succession of layers depicted in the example given below. However, this example is by no means intended to be prescriptive. The main goal of the Layered viewpoint is to provide overview in one diagram. Furthermore, this viewpoint can be used as support for impact of change analysis and performance analysis or for extending the service portfolio.

Table 23: Layered Viewpoint Description

Layered Viewpoint	
Stakeholders	Enterprise, process, application, infrastructure, and domain architects
Concerns	Consistency, reduction of complexity, impact of change, flexibility
Purpose	Designing, deciding, informing
Abstraction Level	Overview
Layer	Business layer, application layer, technology layer (see also Figure 5)
Aspects	Information, behavior, structure (see also Figure 5)

Concepts and Relations

All concepts and all relations.

Example

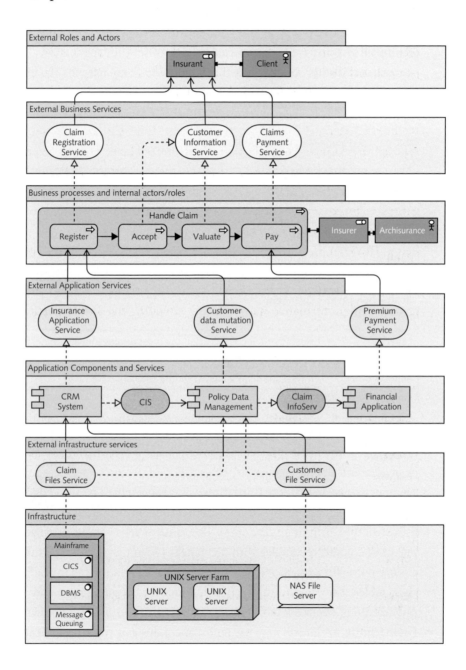

9.4.18 Landscape Map Viewpoint

A landscape map is a matrix that represents a three-dimensional coordinate system that represents architectural relations. The dimensions of the landscape maps can be freely chosen from the architecture that is being modeled. In practice, often dimensions are chosen from different architectural domains; for instance, business functions, application components, and products. Note that a landscape map uses the ArchiMate *concepts*, but not the standard *notation* of these concepts.

Table 24: Landscape Map Viewpoint Description

Landscape Map Viewpoint		
Stakeholders	Enterprise architects, top managers: CEO, CIO	
Concerns	Readability, management and reduction of complexity, comparison of alternatives	
Purpose	Deciding	
Abstraction Level	Overview	
Layer	Business layer, application layer, technology layer (see also Figure 5)	
Aspects	Information, behavior, structure (see also Figure 5)	

In most cases, the vertical axis represents behavior like business processes or functions; the horizontal axis represents "cases" for which those functions or processes must be executed, such as different products, services market segments, or scenarios; the third dimension represented by the cells of the matrix is used for assigning resources like information systems, infrastructure, or human resources. The value of cells can be visualized by means of colored rectangles with text labels. Obviously, landscape maps are a more powerful and expressive representation of relations than traditional cross tables. They provide a practical manner for the generation and publication of overview tables for managers, process, and system owners. Furthermore, architects may use landscape maps as a resource allocation instrument and as an analysis tool for the detection of patterns and changes in this allocation.

Concepts and Relations

All concepts and relations.

Example

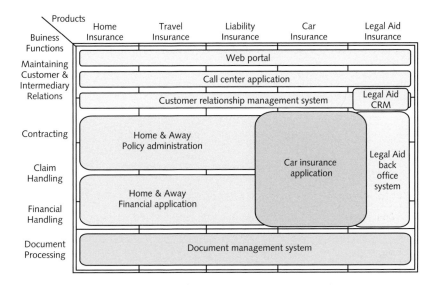

Chapter 10
Language Extension Mechanisms

Every specific purpose and usage of an architecture modeling language brings about its own specific demands on the language. Yet, it should be possible to use a language for only a limited, though non-specific, modeling purpose. Therefore, the ArchiMate core language, embedded in the ArchiMate metamodel, as described in Chapters 3 to 7, contains only the basic concepts and relationships that serve general enterprise architecture modeling purposes. However, the language should also be able to facilitate, through extension mechanisms, specialized, or domain-specific purposes, such as:

- Support for specific types of model analysis
- Support the communication of architectures
- Capture the specifics of a certain application domain (e.g., the financial sector)

The argument behind this statement is to provide a means to allow extensions of the core language that are tailored towards such specific domains or applications, without burdening the core with a lot of additional concepts and notation which most people would barely use. The remainder of this section is devoted to a number of possible extensions mechanisms that, in addition to the core, are or can become part of the ArchiMate language.

10.1 Adding Attributes to ArchiMate Concepts and Relations

As said before, the core of ArchiMate contains only the concepts and relationships that are necessary for general architecture modeling. However, users might want to be able to, for example, perform model-based performance or cost calculations, or to attach supplementary information (textual, numerical, etc.) to the model elements. A simple way to enrich ArchiMate concepts and relationships in a generic way is to add supplementary information by means of a "profiling" specialization mechanism (see also [13]). A *profile* is a data structure which can be defined separate from the ArchiMate language, but can be dynamically coupled with concepts or relationships; i.e., the user of the language is free to decide whether and when the assignment of a profile to a model element is necessary. Profiles can be specified as sets of typed attributes, by means of a profile definition language. Each of these attributes may have a default value that can be changed by the user.

We can distinguish two types of profiles:

- *Pre-defined profiles:* These are profiles that have a predefined attribute structure and can be implemented beforehand in any tool supporting the ArchiMate language. Examples of such profiles are sets of attributes for ArchiMate concepts and relationships that have to be specified in order to execute common types of analysis.
- *User-defined profiles:* Through a profile definition language, the user is able to define new profiles, thus extending the definition of ArchiMate concepts or relationships with supplementary attribute sets.

Example

Table 25 below shows possible profiles with input attributes needed for certain types of cost and performance analysis of architecture models [21]. Each "used by" relationship may have a weight (indicating the average number of uses); each (business, application, or infrastructure) "service" may have fixed and variable costs and an (average) service time; and each structure element (e.g., business role, business actor, application component, device) may have fixed and variable costs and a capacity.

Table 25: Profile Example

"Used By" Profile		"Service" Profile		"Structure Element" Profile	
Attribute	**Type**	**Attribute**	**Type**	**Attribute**	**Type**
Weight	Real	Fixed cost	Currency	Fixed cost	Currency
		Variable cost	Currency	Variable cost	Currency
		Service time	Time	Capacity	Integer

10.2 Specialization of Concepts

Specialization is a simple and powerful way to define new concepts based on the existing ones. Specialized concepts inherit the properties of their "parent" concepts, but additional restrictions with respect to their use may apply. For example, some of the relationships that apply for the "parent" concept may not be allowed for the specialization. A specialized concept strongly resembles a stereotype as it is used in UML. Specialization of concepts provides extra flexibility, as it allows organizations or individual users to customize the language to their own preferences and needs, while the underlying precise definition of the concepts is conserved. This also implies that analysis and visualization techniques developed for the ArchiMate language still apply when the specialized concepts are used.

Figure 55 shows a number of examples of concept specializations that have proven to be useful in several practical cases.

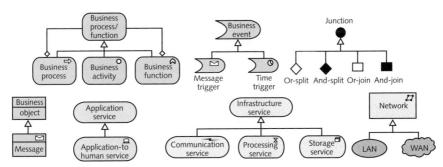

Figure 55: More Examples of Specialized Concepts

Also, the concepts in the layer-specific metamodels can be considered specializations of the concepts in the generic metamodel of Chapter 3.

As the above examples indicate, we may introduce a new graphical notation for a specialized concept, but usually with a resemblance to the notation of the parent concept; e.g., by adding or changing the icon. It is also possible to use a <<stereotype>>-notation as in UML. Finally, for a specialized concept, certain attributes may be predefined, as described in the previous section.

Chapter 11

Future Directions

The current version of the ArchiMate language as specified in this Technical Standard has a strong focus on describing the operational aspects of an enterprise. Although the aim is to keep the core of the language relatively small, a number of directions for extending the language, as well as more advanced tool support for inherent features of ArchiMate models, can be envisaged. In this chapter, we identify some likely extensions for future versions of the language and associated tool support. Furthermore, we look at the construction of the language itself, which lends itself to relatively easy generalization and extension.

11.1 Extending and Refining the Concepts

In the practical use of ArchiMate, four fields have been identified in which a future extension of the language may be advisable:

- Strategy, goals, principles, and requirements
- Evolution and realization of architectures
- The design process
- Architecture-level predictions

11.1.1 Strategy, Goals, Principles, and Requirements

Recall the definition of "architecture" of ISO/IEC 42010:2007 [2]:

"The fundamental organization of a system, embodied in its components, their relationships to each other and the environment, and the principles governing its design and evolution."

In the current version of ArchiMate, the emphasis is on concepts related to the first part of this definition, which we could call the "extensional" aspects of the enterprise; i.e., its appearance as an operational entity. The "intentional" aspects – i.e., its business goals, principles, policies, reasons, rules, requirements, and other aspects that influence, guide, and constrain its design and operation – are less well covered. This would be approximately equivalent to the "Why" column of the Zachman framework [5], which was intentionally left out of scope in the design of ArchiMate 1.0.

Thus, an obvious extension is the introduction of concepts to model different kinds of intentionality, both of the enterprise as a whole (e.g., business goals), and of the translation of these into restrictions on the architectural design itself (e.g., requirements, principles, rules, and constraints).

TOGAF makes a distinction between "enterprise principles" (which are closely related to business goals), "IT principles", and "architecture principles". Architecture principles can be either principles governing the architecture itself, the process by which it is created, or principles governing the architecture's implementation. Architecture principles may pertain to the different types of architecture that TOGAF distinguishes; i.e., principles can be classified based on their impact on the business, data, application, or technology architecture.

A topic that is closely related to principles is the use of business rules, which can be seen as a realization of principles. Business rules separate the business logic from the processes, or put constraints on the business operations. Business can be specified not only at the detailed design level and the execution level (i.e., rules that can be directly executed by a rule engine), but also at the architecture level [22].

11.1.2 Evolution and Realization

Second, an architecture description and the ensuing enterprise is not a static, one-shot affair. Its evolution also needs to be supported. This entails adding concepts for describing changes – for example, to define different versions of architecture elements – and the relation over time between different architecture stages; e.g., plateaus or (current and future) states.

Furthermore, these changes are to be brought about in an orderly fashion: they need to have a clear relationship with the organizational goals, principles, and rationale mentioned before, and they should be realized by means of a coherent portfolio of programs and projects that take the enterprise from one stage to another [29]. Hence, the link between ArchiMate models and portfolio management needs to be addressed in a future version of the language. This could also provide an important management tool for overseeing the realization of architectural plans, a kind of "management dashboard", enabling informed governance.

11.1.3 Design Process

Third, the language could provide additional support for the early stages of the architecture development process. In these early stages, architects will often use informal, sketchy, and incomplete models that later evolve into formally correct ArchiMate models. Hence, a relaxation of formal correctness criteria in the early design stages might be in order. Support for this design evolution will of course be closely related to the concepts envisaged in the previous section, since design decisions are guided by goals, principles, and requirements, and the design process is instrumental to the evolution of the architecture.

Of course, the concepts for the three areas mentioned need to be highly integrated: goals, principles, and requirements guide the architecture evolution, which in turn is operationalized in part by the design process. Full traceability from high-level goals via design decisions down to the resulting architecture elements is desirable.

11.1.4 Architecture-Level Predictions

When you have to make the business case for different architecture alternatives, it is useful to be able to predict different qualities of the alternatives: performance, costs, reliability, etc., as illustrated for example in [21]. This requires different computational models, from where to some extent existing results can be borrowed; e.g., petri nets [23], system dynamics [24], operations research, [25], etc. Where [21] illustrated the potential of architecture-level predictions, more work is needed to make it feasible to include this in ArchiMate tooling.

11.1.5 Other Improvements

Next to the extensions in the areas mentioned above, some definitions of language concepts might also be improved and clarified. For example, the grouping concept could be given more explicit semantics. In practical use, some concepts have been used to good effect for other purposes than strictly intended; their future definitions may be updated to account for such usage.

11.2 Linking to Other Modeling Languages and Frameworks

Practical experience shows that ArchiMate is a useful and practicable tool for high-level enterprise architecture modeling. However, it intentionally does not cover the lower levels of detail of architecture and design for various domains. Rather, it intends to link to more specialized modeling languages for this. In the ArchiMate language definition, several application and technology concepts have a clear link to UML 2.0 [8], [12], as has been described in the previous sections. Similarly, business process concepts are closely related to the Business Process Modeling Notation (BPMN) [26].

Next to these two languages, there are several other relevant modeling techniques. In particular, this includes a number of other OMG standards: the Business Motivation Model (BMM) [27] for specifying the rationale behind an architecture; the Semantics of Business Vocabulary and Business Rules (SBVR) standard [28] for defining natural-language descriptions of business entities; the Business Process Definition Metamodel (BPDM) [29] for specifying detailed business process concepts. Furthermore, the link between ArchiMate and modeling techniques such as i* [30] for requirements modeling, DEMO [10] for transactional models, and e3value [31] for business and value networks could be explored further.

The links between these languages and ArchiMate need to be formally specified, possibly in the form of model transformations as defined in the Model-Driven Architecture (MDA) and the Queries, Views, & Transformations (QVT) transformation language [32]. Preferably, a generic linking mechanism based on these transformations will be defined that can also be used to relate to other, not yet identified languages.

Next to modeling languages, there is also a plethora of architecture frameworks to which ArchiMate can be related. First, there are of course the Zachman [5] and TOGAF [4] frameworks. Other relevant frameworks and conceptual models include DoDAF [33], MoDAF [33], FEA [34], and the CBDI SAE metamodel for SOA [35].

11.3 How to Proceed

Extensions and improvements to the current version of the language need of course to be approached with caution. A central principle in creating a new language version will be backwards compatibility: a correct model expressed in ArchiMate 1.0 will still be a correct model in future language versions. Luckily, the design of the ArchiMate language already provides us with an important advantage. Its metamodel is constructed in a stratified fashion, starting from a core set of concepts that are specialized for each of the different layers (business, application, technology) of the language (see Figure 2). This allows us to define a future version of the language explicitly in two strata, akin to the Infrastructure and Superstructure definitions of UML 2.0 [8], [12]. The current version of the language could then be viewed as a specific instantiation (i.e., Superstructure) of the ArchiMate 2.0 core (i.e., Infrastructure). Hence, ArchiMate 1.0 models will be fully correct ArchiMate 2.0 as well.

To make this happen, first a slight clean-up of the current core concepts (the Infrastructure) is needed, resulting in a version 1.1 of the language. Since these concepts are invisible to language users, who only work with the specializations at each layer, the impact of this will be minimal. Based on this version 1.1, a version 2.0 may then be defined that addresses one or more of the extensions suggested above.

A

Summary of Language Notation

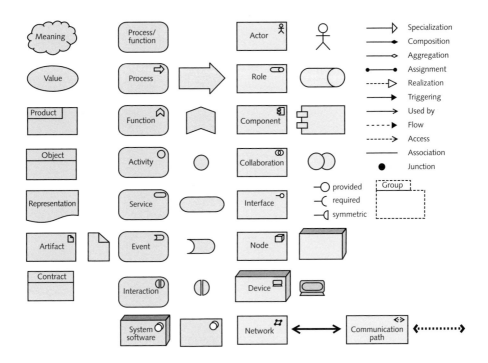

B

Overview of Relationships

	Junction	Business activity	Business event	Business interaction	Business process	Business actor	Business interface	Business collab.	Business role	Business function	Contract	Product	Business Service	Value	Business object	Representation	Meaning
Junction	ft	ft	ft	ft	ft	ft	ft	ft	ft	ft			ft				
Business activity	ft	fostu	fotu	fotu	fotu	ou	ou	ou	ou	fotu	ao	oru	oru	o	ao	ao	o
Business event	ft	fot	cfgost	fot	fot	o	o	o	o	fot	ao	o	o	o	ao	ao	o
Business interaction	ft	fotu	fotu	cfgostu	fotu	ou	ou	ou	ou	fotu	ao	oru	oru	o	ao	ao	o
Business process	ft	cfgotu	cfgotu	fotu	cfgostu	ou	ou	ou	ou	cfgotu	ao	oru	oru	o	ao	ao	o
Business actor	ft	iou	iou	ou	iou	cfgostu	fiotu	cfgiostu	cfgiostu	fiou	au	oru	ioru	o	ao	ao	o
Business interface	ft	ou	ou	ou	ou	fotu	cfgostu	fotu	fotu	ou	ao	oru	iou	o	ao	ao	o
Business-collaboration	ft	iou	iou	iou	iou	cfgostu	cfgiotu	cfgiostu	cfgiostu	fiou	ao	oru	ioru	o	ao	ao	o
Business role	ft	iou	iou	ou	iou	cfgostu	cfgiotu	cfgiostu	cfgiostu	flou	ao	oru	ioru	o	ao	ao	o
Business function	ft	cfgotu	cfgotu	fotu	cfgotu	fou	ou	fou	fou	cfgostu	ao	oru	oru	o	ao	ao	o
Contract		o	o	o	o	o	o	ou	o	o	cgos	o	o	o	cgos	o	o
Product		ou	ou	ou	ou	ou	ou	ou	ou	ou	ago	cgosu	gou	o	ao	ao	o
Business service		ou	ou	ou	ou	ou	ou	o	ou	ou	ao	ou	cfgostu	o	ao	ao	o
Value		o	o	o	o	o	o	o	o	o	o	o	o	cgos	o	o	o
Business object		o	o	o	o	o	o	o	o	o	cgos	o	o	o	cgos	cgos	o
Representation		o	o	o	o	o	o	o	o	o	or	o	o	o	or	cgos	cgos
Meaning		o	o	o	o	o	o	o	o	o	o	o	o	o	o	o	o

Relationships:

(a)ccess	ass(i)gnment	(c)omposition	(r)ealization	(t)riggering
a(g)gregation	ass(o)ciation	(f)low	(s)pecialization	(u)sed by

	Junction	Business activity	Business event	Business interaction	Business process	Business actor	Business interface	Business collab.	Business role	Business function	Contract	Product	Business Service	Value	Business object	Representation	Meaning
Application collaboration	ft	iou	iou	iou	iou	fotu	fotu	fotu	fotu	iou	ao	oru	ioru	o	ao	ao	o
Application component	ft	iou	iou	ou	iou	fotu	fotu	fotu	fotu	iou	ao	oru	ioru	o	ao	ao	o
Application function	ft	ou	ou	ou	ou	ou	ou	ou	ou	ou	ao	ou	ou	o	ao	ao	o
Application interaction	ft	ou	ou	ou	ou	ou	ou	ou	ou	ou	ao	ou	ou	o	ao	ao	o
Application interface	ft	ou	ou	ou	ou	fotu	fotu	fotu	fotu	ou	ao	ou	iou	o	ao	ao	o
Application service	ft	ou	ou	ou	ou	ou	ou	ou	ou	ou	ao	ou	fotu	o	ao	ao	o
Data object		o	o	o	o	o	o	o	o	o	or	o	o	o	or	o	o
Artifact		o	o	o	o	o	o	o	o	o	aor	or	o	o	aor	ao	o
Communiction path		o	o	o	o	o	o	o	o	o	o	o	o	o	o	o	o
Device	ft	ou	ou	ou	ou	ou	ou	ou	ou	ou	ao	ou	ou	o	ao	ao	o
Node	ft	ou	ou	ou	ou	ou	ou	ou	ou	ou	ao	ou	ou	o	ao	ao	o
Infrastructure interface	ft	ou	ou	ou	ou	ou	ou	ou	ou	ou	ao	ou	ou	o	ao	ao	o
Network	ft	o	o	o	o	o	o	o	o	o	o	o	o	o	o	ao	o
Infrastructure service	ft	ou	ou	ou	ou	ou	ou	ou	ou	ou	ao	ou	ou	o	ao	ao	o
System software	ft	ou	ou	ou	ou	ou	ou	ou	ou	ou	ao	ou	ou	o	ao	ao	o

Relationships:

(a)ccess	ass(i)gnment	(c)omposition	(r)ealization	(t)riggering
a(g)gregation	ass(o)ciation	(f)low	(s)pecialization	(u)sed by

	Applic. collaboration	Applic. component	Applic. function	Applic. interaction	Applic. interface	Applic. service	Data object	Artifact	Commun. path	Device	Node	Infrastr. interface	Network	Infrastr. service	System sofware
Junction	ft	ft	ft	ft	ft	ft				ft	ft	ft		ft	ft
Business activity	ou	ou	ou	ou	ou	oru	ao	o	o	o	o	o	o	o	o
Business event	o	o	o	o	o	o	o	o	o	o	o	o	o	o	o
Business interaction	ou	ou	ou	ou	ou	oru	ao	o	o	o	o	o	o	o	o
Business process	ou	ou	ou	ou	ou	oru	ao	o	o	o	o	o	o	o	o
Business actor	fotu	fotu	ou	ou	fotu	oru	ao	o	o	o	o	o	o	o	o
Business interface	fotu	fotu	ou	ou	fotu	oru	ao	o	o	o	o	o	o	o	o
Business collaboration	fotu	fotu	ou	ou	fotu	oru	ao	o	o	o	o	o	o	o	o
Business role	fotu	fotu	ou	ou	fotu	oru	ao	o	o	o	o	o	o	o	o
Business fuction	ou	ou	ou	ou	ou	oru	ao	o	o	o	o	o	o	o	o
Contract	o	o	o	o	o	o	o	o	o	o	o	o	o	o	o
Product	ou	ou	ou	ou	ou	gou	ao	o	o	o	o	o	o	o	o
Business service	ou	ou	ou	ou	ou	fotu	ao	o	o	o	o	o	o	o	o
Value	o	o	o	o	o	o	o	o	o	o	o	o	o	o	o
Business object	o	o	o	o	o	o	o	o	o	o	o	o	o	o	o
Representation	o	o	o	o	o	o	o	o	o	o	o	o	o	o	o
Meaning	o	o	o	o	o	o	o	o	o	o	o	o	o	o	o

Relationships:

(a)ccess	ass(i)gnment	(c)omposition	(t)riggering
a(g)gregation	ass(o)ciation	(f)low	(u)sed by
		(r)ealization	
		(s)pecialization	

	Applic. collaboration	Applic. component	Applic. function	Applic. interaction	Applic. interface	Applic. service	Data object	Artifact	Commun. path	Device	Node	Infrastr. interface	Network	Infrastr. service	System sofware
Application collaboration	cfgostu	cfgostu	iou	iou	cfgotu	ioru	ao	o	o	o	o	o	o	o	o
Application component	cfgostu	cfgostu	iou	ou	cfgotu	ioru	ao	o	o	o	o	o	o	o	o
Application function	ou	ou	cfgostu	fotu	ou	oru	ao	o	o	o	o	o	o	o	o
Application interaction	ou	ou	fotu	cfgostu	ou	oru	ao	o	o	o	o	o	o	o	o
application interface	fotu	fotu	ou	ou	cfgostu	iou	ao	o	o	o	o	o	o	o	o
Application servicce	ou	ou	ou	ou	ou	cfgostu	ao	o	o	o	o	o	o	o	o
Data object	o	o	o	o	o	o	cgos	o	o	o	o	o	o	o	o
Artifact	oru	oru	oru	oru	oru	oru	aor	cgos	o	o	o	o	o	o	o
Communication path	o	o	o	o	o	o	o	o	cgos	o	o	o	o	o	o
Device	ou	ou	ou	ou	ou	ou	ao	aiou	ioru	cfgostu	cfgostu	cfgotu	iou	ioru	cfgiostu
Noode	ou	ou	ou	ou	ou	ou	ao	aiou	ioru	cfgostu	cfgostu	cfgotu	iou	ioru	cfgiostu
Infrastructure interface	ou	ou	ou	ou	ou	ou	ao	aou	ou	fotu	fotu	cfgostu	iou	iou	fotu
Network	o	o	o	o	o	o	o	o	or	o	o	o	cgos	o	o
Infrastructure service	ou	ou	ou	ou	ou	ou	ao	aou	ou	ou	ou	ou	ou	cfgostu	ou
System software	ou	ou	ou	ou	ou	ou	ao	aiou	ioru	cfgostu	cfgostu	cfgotu	iou	ioru	cfgiostu

Relationships:

(a)ccess	ass(i)gnment	(c)omposition	(t)riggering
a(g)gregation	ass(o)ciation	(f)low	(u)sed by
		(r)ealization	
		(s)pecialization	

Index